Thinking About Morality

Thinking About Morality

Bernie Koenig

HAMILTON BOOKS
Lanham • Boulder • New York • London

Published by Hamilton Books
An imprint of The Rowman & Littlefield Publishing Group, Inc.
4501 Forbes Boulevard, Suite 200, Lanham, Maryland 20706
www.rowman.com

6 Tinworth Street, London SE11 5AL, United Kingdom

Copyright © 2021 The Rowman & Littlefield Publishing Group, Inc.

All rights reserved. No part of this book may be reproduced in any form or by any electronic or mechanical means, including information storage and retrieval systems, without written permission from the publisher, except by a reviewer who may quote passages in a review.

British Library Cataloguing in Publication Information Available

Library of Congress Cataloging-in-Publication Data:

Names: Koenig, Bernie, 1943- author.
Title: Thinking about morality / Bernie Koenig.
Description: Lanham : Hamilton Books, 2021. | Includes bibliographical
  references and index.
Identifiers: LCCN 2020055491 (print) | LCCN 2020055492 (ebook) | ISBN
  9780761872016 (paperback) | ISBN 9780761872023 (ebook)
Subjects: LCSH: Ethics. | Reasoning. | Thought and thinking.
Classification: LCC BJ1012 .K574 2021 (print) | LCC BJ1012 (ebook) | DDC
  170—dc23
LC record available at https://lccn.loc.gov/2020055491
LC ebook record available at https://lccn.loc.gov/2020055492

I would like to dedicate this book to the memory of
BERNARD HODGSON
Who always encouraged my writing

Contents

Preface ix

Introduction 1

1 Origins of Values 15
2 Multiculturalism 41
3 Sex and Gender 57
4 Issues of Life and Death: Abortion and Euthanasia 79
5 Slavery, Human Trafficking and Prostitution 99
6 The Environment 113
7 Guns 125
8 Drugs 133
9 The Teaching of Art 141

Concluding Remarks 147

Bibliography 149

Index 155

About the Author 159

Preface

Since my book *Natural Law, Science, and the Social Construction of Reality* was published in 2004 I have done a lot of thinking about moral issues, and about how to think about moral issues.[1] In that time I have read a number of papers at the International Medieval Congress on topics ranging from the relationship between natural law and communitarianism to how the knowledge of today would affect Aquinas's views and to the natural law traditions in Judaism and Islam. I also read papers at other conferences on a variety of issues. One in particular, which will be mentioned later, was on Canadian humorist and economist Stephen Leacock, where I showed that his humorous stories in fact reflected his serious work in economics. I have also been active in various causes and have participated in a number of election campaigns at all levels of government.

As a citizen of a democracy I believe it is important to be well informed, so I have also followed the news on various moral issues, as discussed in the political arena, from abortion, sexual assault, prostitution and human trafficking, to drug use, gun control and immigration and refugee issues. Given my philosophical background, and my knowledge of moral theory I have tried to formulate views on all of these issues. Sometimes it has been easy; sometimes it has been very hard. It has been hard for two very different reasons. One is the complexity of the issue. For example, is prostitution a form of human trafficking, especially when the people in the trade themselves say no? Secondly, the social context of the issue often colors how the issue is discussed—for example, police and judges who too easily dismiss claims of sexual assault because of ingrained views.

As a philosopher I have tried to apply critical thinking to all of these issues. And, given my background in natural law, I always look for relevant information to help resolve issues. After all, natural law is about having a knowledge base to one's values. The main argument of my book was that as knowledge changes, as our understanding of how the world works changes, our values must also change. Thus I have what could be called a knowledge basis for my moral thinking.

I have also been highly influenced by anthropology and psychology. As I recounted in that book, my introduction to this approach to moral theory came from a debate on Hannah Arendt's book, *Eichmann in Jerusalem*, where two psychologists debated Eichmann's situation, not from differing moral perspectives, but from their different views on human nature. I later discovered that this is an approach to natural law.

In thinking about natural law and in participating over the years in the natural law section of the International Medieval Congress, I owe a great debt to Harvey Brown. He introduced me to the Congress, and has encouraged my work in the field.

I would also like to thank various friends and colleagues who have read parts or all of this manuscript and have made many helpful suggestions. I especially want to thank May Lee-Jarvis for her excellent help with editing. And I must mention my wife, Paddy Musson, for both for her comments and her wonderful support.

NOTES

1. Bernie Koenig, Natural Law, Science, and the Social Construction of Reality, (Lanham: University Press of America, 2004)

Introduction

As a philosopher I try to use reason to analyze the issue and the situation in order to arrive at a meaningful conclusion. I also want to phrase my conclusion in a way that the people involved can understand. It is extremely important to do this. It is one thing to have great values and views on issues; it is another to accurately communicate them. What is the point of having a solution to a problem is if no one understands it?

I approach problem solving by trying to break down the issue. I begin by using the subject matter of philosophy: metaphysics, epistemology, axiology and logic. "Meta" means above or beyond or over, thus metaphysics goes beyond what we know about the physical world into areas of speculation, asking questions such as, "Where did the universe come from?" "Why are we here?' and so on. But because we are dealing with metaphysics we really can't know if our answers are correct or not.

But when we apply metaphysics to a moral issue we must ask why it is an issue—where is the conflict? We often see that conflicts in such issues are between old ways of understanding an issue and new knowledge, leading to new ways of understanding the issue. Indeed, the main theme of my book is that in the tradition of natural law, where moral values are derived from an understanding of how people fit into the natural order, as our understanding of the natural order changes, what is natural —what is moral—must also change.

Once we have a clear statement of the issue, we must look to epistemology, the study of knowledge. When we say that we know X or that X is true, we must be able to state the criteria we use to justify those claims. We also look at the role perception plays in knowledge and how language reflects what we know.

When applying epistemology to a moral issue we must look for the relevant knowledge to apply to the issue. For example, in the case of turning off a respirator, we must apply knowledge of the nature of life. For most of human history we used respiratory criteria for determining whether someone was alive or not. Now, because of developments in both medical knowledge and in medical technology, our definitions of life and death are shifting from respiratory to brain functions.

Then we look at the values involved. Axiology is the study of values. What are values, both moral and aesthetic? Are they objective or subjective? Do we learn value language the same way as we learn object language?

When applying axiology to moral questions we must ask how our existing values affect how we see the problem, and whether the knowledge we have learned should lead to changing those values.

And finally, we use logic, which is the study of the process of reasoning, to make connections and arrive at conclusions. Logic is also used to examine the validity of premises, and to look at the reasoning behind arguments. For example, if we look at a question, and make a list of pros and cons for doing something, we will find that some of the reasons hold up well, others may hold up for very specific cases and still others may not hold up at all. If I ask myself why I should get out of bed in the morning, I will say I have to go to work, I have other obligations, I need to eat, and so on. If I say I should not get out of bed because I am sick, or that I am hung over, or that I hate my job, I must then evaluate these reasons. If I am sick it is valid to stay in bed, but once I am well, I will get up. If I stay in bed because I am hung over, I will get out of bed once I am sober. Thus, logic is used not only to examine reasoning, but to evaluate reasons as well.

All of this is to use moral theory. Before continuing, three definitions are needed: we must clearly define the terms moral, ethics, and theory. The meanings and uses of these terms have changed over the years. Morality is about our public behavior; the word has the same root as "mores," the conventions of a community. When we break a rule governing public behavior it is usually judged in terms of the consequences. Ethics has always been about how we carry out our specific social roles. I have certain obligations or duties in my role as a teacher, doctor, soldier, etc. Breaking those obligations is usually seen in terms of intent and motive. What did I hope to achieve by behaving in that way, and why would I think of behaving in that way? But in the nineteenth century, in the legal system, judges started asking about intent regarding moral issues in order to judge the consequences. If I set out to harm someone I would be treated one way, but if I harmed someone but did not set out to do so, I would be treated another way. Because of this trend, the terms morals and ethics tended to become interchangeable. And today, the dictionary defines ethics as a system of morality, completely turning the meanings around. In this work, I will try to use these terms in their traditional ways.

Now to define "theory." I have long argued that theory is the most misused word in our language. Most people use the word theory where they should use the word hypothesis. Theories are all too often contrasted with knowledge, as in "that is only a theory." When a detective says she has a theory as to who did it, she should be saying that she has a hypothesis. A hypothesis is an educated guess. In science it is a beginning point for experimentation. A theory is in fact a form of explanation. As Wilfrid Sellars puts it, "Theories explain laws by explaining why the objects of the domain in question obey the laws that they do to the extent that they do."[1] A textbook example is explaining how water turns to steam. We put a pot of water on a fire, go away for a while, and when we return we find no water in the pot. Do we say that water spirits took the water away? Then we do another experiment and cover the pot. When we come back we see that most of the water is in the pot but there is some water on the inside of the cover. In a third experiment we put a straw through the cover and lead the straw to an empty pot. After a while we see that all the water is now in the second pot.

So instead of talking about water spirits, we use our understanding of the molecular structure of things. We know that water is made up of hydrogen and oxygen. We also know that, according to Boyle's law, when a gas is heated it expands, and when cooled it contracts. From atomic theory we know that gases behave this way because the components of the atoms that make up the molecules move faster when heated and when they move faster they move in larger arcs, thus they expand. We call it atomic theory because we do not directly see the atoms expand. But we know they exist and use them to explain what we do observe.

So what is a moral theory? Simply put, a moral theory is an attempt to explain why we should or should not behave in certain ways, and/or it provides basic principles to help us make such choices. It is also used to evaluate behavior.

Moral concepts come from all types of places, cultures, religions, and political forces. For example, in Ancient Greece, religion had no bearing on morality. Morality was part of the culture. Of course, there were gods and goddesses, but they had their own lives. They could, and did, interfere in human affairs, but not to bring about moral beliefs.

In various indigenous cultures alive today, a similar situation exists. If you were to ask a Native Canadian what his or her religion was, you would probably get a blank stare in response since the native belief system is part and parcel of their daily culture. Religion is not an addition to the culture. Creation stories lead to moral values and precepts on how to live.

But mainly in the West, religion has become separated from culture, or has been added on to it. While Judaism and Islam arose out of cultures, Christianity was always an imposed belief system. What makes all three religions similar when it comes to morality is the concept of "natural law." While there are many different definitions of natural law, and there are secular as well as religious views of natural law, all have in common the relationship between knowledge and values. And, of course, in religious views, God plays a role in giving the law.

What I have found interesting in researching the natural law traditions in all three religions is that the concept of revelation, where God is responsible for providing the knowledge of what is natural, and that the commentaries, which endeavor to makes sense of the revelations, reflect the influence of the Ancient Greek philosophers, especially that of Plato and Aristotle. In Judaism what is known as The Old Testament was put together late in the fifth century B.C.E. and most if not all scholars of the period agree there is a strong Hellenic influence in how the stories are told.[2] Christianity arose in the Hellenic world while the Roman Empire was at its height, and Islam developed in a part of the world where Aristotle had actually taught hundreds of years earlier. My point here is that the major philosophical discussions, which largely constitute the body of natural law theory, are based on the writings of these Greek philosophers, even if each religion takes a different approach to the subject.

In all cases, though, natural law theory can be described as first coming to an understanding of the natural order, i.e., how the world works. Next is the understanding of what it means to be human. Then the human is placed in the natural order, and from the interaction we derive what is natural, i.e., what is moral. The added dimension in religious approaches to natural law includes the concept of purposeful creation. Thus discovering what is natural involves, in part, understanding the nature of creation.

The big debate in Islam is over the nature of God. The main thrust of the debate was over the issue of free will or divine determination. As Majid Fakhry points out,[3] the two main groups involved in the debate were the Asherites and the Mu'tazilites, the former believing in divine determination and the latter, believing in free will, seeing the need for philosophical commentary on religious writings.

The view of the Ashherites that everything was divinely determined led the Mu'tazilites to argue that this would imply that the evil in the world was also by divine determination, and since God was understood as Good, this could not be the case. Thus the Mu'tazilites argued that free will was the cause of evil and that philosophical reflection of religious writings was necessary to make sense of the moral implications of those writings.

One can argue that the Asherite position was influenced by Plato, given his absolutist views on the nature of the universe, and that the Mu'tazilites were influenced by the practical reasoning of Aristotle.

To take this discussion into contemporary terms I would like to conclude with a look at a paper I discovered online, regarding the relationship between natural law and Shari'a law. This paper, presented by Imad-ad-Dean Ahmad of the Minaret of Freedom Institute to the Institute of Freedom's Summer Institute, August third, 2009.[4]

He points out that natural law applies not only to laws of nature—physics—but also to human nature. In this context Ahmed argues that,

> It is by an acknowledgement of the connection between human nature and the laws governing man that reason can be understood to play a role in the understanding of the law. In Shia jurisprudence, reason is identified as a source of the law.

And that,

> The upshot of this analysis is not to deny the possibility of science, but to transform it from an exercise in mere logic into a study of the divine will, i.e., of God's signs in the heavens and on the earth. In the same way the social sciences become the study of God's signs in ourselves. That is to say, the social sciences are the study of laws of human nature, which is, like the nature of physical reality, God-given. As the laws that govern human behavior are God given, the knowledge of revelation is relevant to its study.

Thus, Islam is decidedly not anti science, since scientific knowledge constitutes our understanding of nature, which then forms the basis of God's laws.

So in conclusion, reason and empirical knowledge—scientific knowledge—must play a role in how we make sense of religious writings, as our knowledge changes and our social structures change. But, ultimately, the source of natural law in Islam, as in other religions, is divine revelation.

In Judaism, the main theorist was Moses Maimonides, who was influenced by Aristotle. As he states in Book 111 Chapter 27 of the *Guide for the Perplexed*,[5]

> The general object of the law is twofold: The well being of the soul, and the well being of the body. The well being of the soul is promoted by correct opinions communicated to the people according to their capacity . . . The well-being of the body is established by proper management of the relations in which we live one to another . . . it is also treated in the law and most minutely, because the well being of the soul can only be obtained after that of the body has been secured . . .
>
> The second perfection of man consists in his becoming an actually intelligent being i.e. he knows about the things in existence all that a person perfectly developed is capable of knowing.

> The true Law, which as we said, is one, and beside which there is no other Law, viz, the Law of our teacher Moses, has for its purpose to give us the twofold perfection. It aims first at establishing good relations among men. . . Secondly it seeks to train us in faith, and to impart correct and true opinions when the intellect is sufficiently developed.

So, as I read Maimonides, the basis of law is LAW writ large, the law handed down from God to man through revelation. But man must use his intellect to make sense of the law and use the law to establish proper relationships and political institutions. Thus, though the Law is presented through revelation, and with the whole notion of purposeful creation, mankind learns his role in that creation. When it comes to specifics, we must use our intellect—our reason—to apply the Law to specific situations, hence the use of parables to teach the Law.

In Christianity, the main natural law theorist is Aquinas, who quotes Aristotle throughout his work. His view on the subject is perhaps the most developed of all three, partly because he was influenced by the writings of Averroes and Maimonides. As Aquinas says,[6]

> . . .law is nothing but a dictate of practical reason issued by a sovereign who governs a complete community. Granted that the world is ruled by divine providence. . .it is evident that the whole community of the universe is governed by God's mind. Therefore the ruling idea of things which exists in God as the effective sovereign of them all has the nature of law. Then since God's mind does not conceive in time, but has an eternal concept. . .it follows that this law should be called eternal.

From this Aquinas derives divine law, and in turn he derives natural law.

Now, as we have seen, the conception of nature all three religions accept is that of the Ancient Greeks. The Earth is at the center of the universe with everything revolving around it. Everything is explained as aspects or combinations of the four elements, earth, water, air, and fire, and changes in the world are explained by the four causes, material, formal, efficient and final. These concepts are all discussed in detail by Aristotle.[7] These causes were used to explain the changes in the physical world, and in human action. For Aristotle, as for the three religions, behavior is teleological or purposeful, or goal directed. The goal is the final cause.

The scientific revolution of the sixteenth and seventeenth centuries showed that the Greek view of the world was false. The work of Copernicus and Galileo demonstrated that the sun, not the earth was in the center of the universe. Therefore, as I argued in my book on natural law, since the epistemological foundation of the medieval world view was shown to be false, the religious natural law theories are also false since one is dependent on the other.

After the scientific revolution philosophers attempted to develop theories of morality based on reason. First came concepts of social contract, the most important one in the western world being that of John Locke. The social contract idea was based on how the modern state was developing, especially in regard to challenging the power of the monarchies. Locke argues that political power as "a right of making laws" where men are born into a state of nature—free with the use of reason.

> The state of nature has a law of nature to govern it, which obliges everyone, and reason, which is that law, teaches all mankind, who will but consult it, that being all equal and independent, no one ought to harm another in his life, health, liberty, or possessions.[8]

And this law of nature

> Puts men out of a state of nature into that of a commonwealth, by setting up a judge on earth with authority to determine all the controversies and redress the injuries that may happen to any member of the commonwealth; which judge is the legislative or magistrates appointed by it.[9]

The point here is that the contract—the entering into a commonwealth—is where our rights come from.

Social contract theory is still with us in various forms, and, from a political standpoint, it makes sense, but from a moral standpoint it is lacking in a source of values, other than all people are moral equals. Theoretically a group of people can create any kind of commonwealth or state they choose, so long as everyone in that commonwealth or community is regarded as everyone else's equal. Of course, in Locke's day, even though the purpose of his work was to develop a secular, rational basis for morality, the actual specifics of what was and was not moral still came from religion. The one thing that social contract theory does give us today is a sense of context. We can talk about the way a society is structured, especially from a values standpoint, using social contract theory.

One of the theories that tried to develop a real sense of values was utilitarianism. The idea can be found in many sources, but the philosophers primarily associated with utilitarian theory are Jeremy Bentham and John Stewart Mill. But the work of David Hume must be mentioned as well. Hume is the great empiricist skeptic. He saw morality as attached to the passions, and as such there is no ultimate foundation to morality, but we learn our moral principles through custom and habit, by participating in society. and through education. Morality is about achieving human happiness, and Hume saw this as coming from, "reflections on public interest and utility,"[10] where the principle of utility becomes the basis for justice. Utility is understood in terms of use or function, and we must use our rationality to maximize our utility. But like a good empiricist Hume did not try to state moral values but claimed to describe how people actually behaved. Hume is concerned with actions and consequences, but ultimately everything is about an action's usefulness for bringing about some good for society. This usefulness overcomes self-interest, especially when self-interest is in conflict with the public interest.

Hume was a major influence on Adam Smith. Today we read, or misread, his *Wealth of Nations*,[11] but his earlier work, which should be read as a prolegomenon to *The Wealth of Nations* is *A Theory of Moral Sentiments* where Smith argues that,[12]

> that the market economy will only work if marketeers are concerned about the consequences of their actions on others, for Smith saw the workings of the market in moral terms. Smith's invisible hand was not just a self-regulating mechanism but a moral prescription. Smith talks about the community and how individuals develop concern for others through the development of the notion of sympathy. Following David Hume, Smith acknowledges that we cannot feel the pains of another person, but we can judge another's misfortunes through a comparison to our own pains by changing places in fancy with the sufferer, that we come either to conceive or be affected by what he feels. Smith argues that when trying to understand another person's viewpoint (T)o approve of another man's opinions is to adopt those opinions, and to adopt them is to approve of them.[13]

Smith is famous for his notion of the invisible hand.[14] This was not a fancy but a belief in the rationality of nature, where nature was a self-regulating entity or process. Since people in the state of nature had the use of reason they would come to sympathize or identify with others and act accordingly. The background of Smith's view of morality comes from Locke's notion of rationality and Hume's arguments regarding sentiment as the basis of morality. The important point here is that rationality is understood as an objective process. Everyone will reason the same way. All persons beginning with the same premise will arrive at the same conclusion. If we all pursue our individual interests in a rational manner while recognizing that everyone else is pursuing their interests in a rational manner, we come to understand that everyone's interests are equal. Thus the title of his work *The Theory of Moral Sentiments* is to be taken seriously. The fact that we have sentiments regarding other people limits our actions towards them. Not everything is permissible.

And now we look at Bentham and Mill.[15,16] Bentham begins his work with the role of the individual and by claiming "The community is a fictitious body, composed of the individual persons who are considered as constituting as it were its numbers. The interest of the community then is what?—the sum of the interests of the several members who compose it."[17] But the main part of his work is to explain the principle of utility, which is all about maximizing pleasure and avoiding pain. He talks about the sources of pleasure and pain: the physical, the moral, the political and the religious. The purpose of moral theory for Bentham is to understand these sources so that principles and legislation can be enacted or enforced to maximize pleasure and avoid pain. This is to be done by developing a method of measuring pleasure and pain, so we have information guiding our choices. Such factors include intensity, duration, certainty and the propinquity of the pleasure.

Bentham is aware that our actions affect other people. Thus for Bentham moral theory is ultimately about how our pursuit of pleasure affects other people. And we see this through the consequences of one's actions. Bentham argues that we must be aware of the consequences of our actions since such awareness is the product of a rational decision-making process. The pursuit of pleasure in moral terms must be seen as a rational pursuit. It is the use of rationality that makes the pursuit of pleasure a moral enterprise.

Now we turn to Mill, whose work can be seen as an elaboration or development of Bentham's. It should also be pointed out that Mill wrote *"On Liberty"* and *"On the Subjection of Women"* most likely with Harriet Taylor, who, Mill acknowledged, was a great influence on him. What is important here is their notion of pleasure, which has more to do with the intellect and rational pursuits than anything else. Pleasure is understood in terms of awareness and the use of the intellect. It is not base pleasures but the higher ones that use reason. Thus Mill states: "It is better to be a human being dissatisfied than a pig satisfied; better to be Socrates dissatisfied than a fool satisfied."[18] And Mill uses reason to justify the principle of utility:

> We have now then, an answer to the question of what sort of proof the principle of utility is susceptible. If the opinion which I have now stated is psychologically true—if human nature is so constituted as to desire nothing which is not either a part of happiness or a means of happiness—we can have no other proof, and we require no other, that these are the only things desirable. If so, happiness is the sole end of human action, and the promotion of it is the test by which to judge all human conduct; from whence it necessarily follows that it must be the criterion of morality, since a part is included in the whole.[19]

Utilitarianism is alive and well today in various forms. The most important aspect of it is how we judge how our actions might affect other people. The answer is partly following Smith, to put ourselves in the position of the person who will be affected by our actions. If we are not prepared to accept the consequences of an action then we should not perform that action.

Next comes the work of Immanuel Kant. He saw morality from a sense of duty. While he did not deny that happiness is important—after all if we are not happy we cannot function properly—happiness is not the main concern of morality. Duty is.

> Thus the first proposition of morality is that to have moral worth an action must be performed from duty. The second proposition is: An action performed from duty does not have moral worth in the purpose which is to be achieved through it but in the maxim by which it determined... The third principle, as a consequence of the two preceding, I would express as follows: Duty is the necessity of an action executed from respect for the law.[20]

Thus we must have respect for the moral law. Then the question becomes what this law would look like. It would have to involve universality, thus Kant argues that "I should never act in such a way that I could not also will that my maxim should be a universal law."[21] And he presents another version of this idea by stating that "Act so that you treat humanity, whether in your own person or in that of another, always as an end and never as a means only."[22]

Thus we get from Kant something both very different and very similar to utilitarianism. It is similar in that we must treat all people as our moral equals, which means never doing to others what you could not accept being done to oneself. It is different in that Kant's approach relies on duty rather than on consequences for evaluating the behavior in question. Thus it is the action and the intent and/or motive of the actor that are evaluated.

But when we combine the two views we get a more complete view which uses motive and intent to evaluate consequences, so we can make distinctions between, say, first and second-degree murder and manslaughter. We can ask whether the actor in question set out to harm the other person or not. If the intent was to harm another, then the actor in question broke the moral law by not treating the other person as an equal, or, perhaps, if the actor in question was in a reversed situation, he or she would have accepted being harmed. But still, one could argue that trying to bring harm would appear to be breaking the maxim of not treating someone as and end but as a means.

Today we see both debates about whether Mill or Kant provides the better view, or whether the combined view works best. Indeed I have argued that if we add the notion of consequences to Kant's view, even if we forget about the aim of pleasure or happiness, we still get a more complete moral theory.

But as the twentieth century developed problems arose with these views. One had to do with looking at specific contexts, and the other had to do with development of the women's movement. In the 1980s a view sometimes known as feminist ethics, and other times known as the ethics of care, developed. The primary theorist here is Carol Gilligan.

But before we talk about Gilligan's work, a little background is needed. First we need to briefly look at the work of sociologist Nancy Chodorow, whom Gilligan mentions as an influence. In her book *The Reproduction of Mothering: Psychoanalysis and the Sociology of Gender*, Chodorow demonstrates the difference between sex and gender, where sex is biological but gender is socially constructed, thus arguing against Freud's view that biology is destiny. By changing the way we parent, we can change how we raise our children. Thus we do not have to raise them to fulfill traditional roles.

Next we must discuss the work of Lawrence Kohlberg, whose work stimulated Gilligan. Kohlberg, following the work of Jean Piaget, studied how people reasoned about moral issues. Using questionnaires about how people reasoned, Kohlberg came up with a breakdown of stages of reasoning, ranging from what he called the "pre-moral" level, the level of "Conventional Role Conformity" and finally the "Morality of Self-Accepted Principles." His last category involved the ability to reason abstractly and to apply principles to of conscience as if they were abstract universal principles.

From his survey he found that women tended to reason about moral issues in level two, where women tend to see things in situational terms but men reasoned in level three, thereby concluding that men's moral reasoning abilities are superior to women's.

Gilligan sees this as a great paradox in that is these situational ways of looking at things that provide "the very traits that traditionally have defined the 'goodness' of women, their care for and sensitivity to the needs of others, are those that mark them as deficient in moral development."[23] In other words, women actually do the moral work of our society, so to see their moral decision making as lacking is definitely paradoxical. This is so because Kohlberg's and Piaget's views of morality are based on the study of men's lives. But when we look at women's ways of looking moral issues we see a different approach, not an inferior one.

Gilligan then developed her own questionnaire and found that women relate to specifics more than men. But instead of accepting Kohlberg's view that abstract reasoning on moral issues is superior, Gilligan argued that women's sensitivity to the people affected by decisions was more in line with how they were raised to be nurturers rather than being inferior; they were simply thinking, to quote her title, In a Different Voice, not an inferior one.

The important point is that by contextualizing their reasoning, women tend to try to understand the specifics of a case, rather than just apply abstract principles as if one principle is good for all. Gilligan does not shy away from the use of principles, but as I read her, the principles come after one understands the specifics of a situation, rather than just applying a principle. And this is what leads to the different voice.

What this means is that, after listening to how women think about moral issues, Gilligan sees a shift from thinking about a hierarchy of rights or principles to talking about relationships. After hearing a particular woman's story, Gilligan concludes,

> Perceiving relationships as primary rather than as derived from separation, considering interdependence of people's lives, she envisions "the way we are" and "the way things should be" as a web of connection where "everybody belongs to it, and you all come from it."[24]

The woman in question goes on to describe morality as "the constant tension between being part of something larger and a sort of self-contained entity." The tension becomes the source of moral character and strength."[25]

Thus this different voice is about relationships and context, not just about applying abstract principles to moral questions.

So what does this brief summary of moral theory tell us? All these theories have something to contribute but none is sufficient to do the job we want done.

When evaluating an action we first need to clearly define the issue. We use our metaphysical abilities to carefully analyze what is being evaluated and why it needs to be evaluated. Then, partly thanks to natural law theory, and epistemology, we need to find the appropriate knowledge to help us get a clear sense of the issue. Then we apply value theory. From social contract theory we look at the overall social context of the issue, or of the behavior being evaluated. From ethics of care we look at the specific situation the action was undertaken in. We look at who was affected and how. From utilitarianism we look at the consequences of the action in a more general sense. From Kantian duty theory, in order to make sense of the consequences, we look at intent and motive, which gives us an understanding of what the person in question hoped to achieve through that action, and why that person chose that particular means of achieving that end. And then we use logic to arrive at our conclusions regarding what is moral or how to evaluate a possible case of immoral behavior.

Next we have to look at our own behavior. When contemplating an action, we must think of how our action will affect others. So, we can turn to the old golden rule and make sure we do not do anything that we would not want done to us. In other words, we must look at the consequences of our own actions to see if we would be prepared to accept those consequences if we were on the receiving end of our action. If we can accept those consequences, we can perform that action. If we cannot accept such consequences we must not perform that action.

These concepts, then, give us a thorough way of evaluating actions from both the performer's and the affected person's point of view.

NOTES

1. Sellars, Wilfrid. *Science, Perception and Reality*. (London: Routledge and Kegan Paul, 1963) 123.
2. Friedman, Richard, *Who Wrote the Bible*, (New York: Simon and Schuster, 2019).
3. Fakhry, Majid, Islamic Philosophy, Theology and Mysticism, a Short Introduction, (Oxford: Oneworld publications, 1997)
4. Ahmad, Imad-ad-Dean, "On Natural Law and Shari'ah" Delivered August 3, 2009, Institute to the Institute of Freedom's Summer Institute www.minaret.org.pdf site checked on February 3, 2020.
5. Maimonides, Moses, *The Guide for the Perplexed*, trans by M. Friedlander, (New York: Dover, 1956).
6. Aquinas, St Thomas, *Summa Theologica*, 1a 2ae Question 94, articles 1 and 2 . London Blackfriars, 1963. Translation led by His Eminence Michael Cardinal Browne and the Most Reverend Father Aniceto Fernandez.
7. Aristotle, *The Basic Works of Aristotle*, Edited by Richard McKeon, (New York: Random House, 1941).
8. Locke, John, *An Essay Concerning the True Original, Extent and End of Civil Government*, in Barker, Sir Ernest, *Social Contract*, (London:Oxford University Press, 1960) 5.
9. Locke, *Civil Government*, 52.
10. Hume, David, *An Enquiry Concerning the principles of Morals* ed by I.A. Selby-Bigg, (Oxford: The Clarendon Press, 1967) 258.
11. Smith, Adam, *The Wealth of Nations, The Wealth of Nations*, in Heilbroner, Robert, ed, *The Essential Adam Smith, (* New York: W.W. Norton, 1987) i.
12. Smith, Adam, *The Theory of Moral Sentiments*, in Heilbroner.
13. Smith, *Sentiments*, 70.
14. For a good discussion of this topic see Bernard Hodgson, ed, *The Invisible Hand and the Common Good*, (Berlin: Springer, 2004).
15. Bentham, Jeremy, *An Introduction to the Principles of Morals and Legislation* in Cahn and Markie eds, *Ethics: History, Theory and Contemporary Issues* (New York: Oxford University Press, 1998).
16. Mill, John Stuart, *Utilitarianism* in Cahn and Markie.
17. Bentham, 39.
18. Mill, 348.
19. Mill 365.
20. Kant, Immanuel, *Foundations of the Metaphysics of Morals*, translated by Lewis White Beck, (Indianapolis, The Liberal Arts Press, 1959) 16.

21. Kant, 18.
22. Kant, 47.
23. Gilligan, Carol, *In a Different Voice: Psychological Theory and Women's Development*, (Cambridge: Harvard University Press, 1982) 18.
24. Gilligan, 57.
25. Gilligan, 57.

Chapter One

The Origins of Values

In the introduction I raised two issues which I want to pursue in this section. The first is a moral theory based on knowledge, and the second is the idea of a community as the basis of that moral knowledge. Most knowledge based moral theories are usually put into the category of natural law theories, since the knowledge in question would be about the way the world works—the natural order—and how people fit into that order, or how that knowledge is used in formulating moral values. When we understand how communities develop, we also get an understanding of how the structure of the community leads to the development of the communities' moral values.

People are social beings and they live in communities. So part of our understanding of the natural order is to understand how communities develop and how they function. Recall Locke's argument that it is the creation of a community through the social contract that defines our basic values and our basic rights. Thus knowing how communities form and function is important in understanding how moral values develop. In order to develop this understanding we must turn to a range of information from evolution, anthropology, and psychology. Included in this exploration we will look at the work of Darwin, Freud, and Marvin Harris. We shall begin with Darwin.

Darwin's theory explains the evolutionary process, using the concept of natural selection. The story of how Darwin formulated these concepts is well known. As science officer on the Beagle he observed variations in the same species of various animals and realized these differences were adaptations to insure survival in different environments.

> Natural Selection acts exclusively by the preservation and accumulation of Variations, which are beneficial under the organic and inorganic conditions to which each creature is exposed at all periods of life. The ultimate result is

that each creature tends to become more and more improved in relation to its conditions. This improvement inevitably leads to the gradual advancement of the organization of the greater number of living beings throughout the world.[1]

The basic evidence for the truth of evolution includes geological and fossil evidence, the diversity of life around the world, our vestigial organs, such as our tail bones and finger nails, sexual selection, the study of embryology along with developments in the human genome, which also shows the genetic similarity between humans and other species.[2]

Darwin knew that sex played a major role in inheritance, but the knowledge of the day did not understand the biological mechanisms of heredity. It is one of the great ironies of history that shortly after Darwin published *The Origin of Species*, Gregor Mendel discovered the basis laws of heredity. The second irony is that the science of the day was not prepared to accept Mendel's work.

Mendel developed a statistical method for determining the heredity of characteristics. As Nobel Laureate in biology Francois Jacob states, "The symbolic interpretation of the results in some way becomes the hinge between theory and experiment. It permits hypotheses to be formulated easily from the observed distributions; and it leads to predictions that then can be experimentally tested."[3] Jacob goes on to say that his audience "was surprised that arithmetic and calculation of probabilities entered the equation of heredity."[4] But some thirty-five years later, science finally caught up with Mendel and his work was properly appreciated.

But evolution is not only about biology and sexual reproduction. Evolution also occurs through other mechanisms such as non-cellular transmission of traits, behaviors, and symbolic transmission through communication. Thus where and how species live, how they are organized and how they communicate all play a role in the evolutionary process.[5]

Darwin's influence is incalculable. But one of the first people who really tried to apply evolution to understanding human behavior was Sigmund Freud. In his career, Freud attempted to do five things. The first, given his background in neurology, was to find a biological basis for all human behavior. He started on this project early on but due to his clinical work he never returned to it.

In his clinical work he attempted to understand the various symptoms that were presented to him. He found that in order to understand where the symptoms came from, or to understand what they were symptoms of, he had to develop a complete concept of what it is to be a person. Then he developed the method known as psychoanalysis, or the talking cure, where patients had to come to a realization themselves, with the aid of the therapist, as to what they were going through, and why. And finally Freud tried to develop a theory of society.

With regard to dealing with the symptoms of the day, Freud was completely successful. He developed an understanding of what led to those symptoms and was able to cure his patients. Regarding his theory of a person, he was largely correct in seeing that we are first biological beings, then we become socialized and then we develop a sense of self.

Today the talking cure is a bit out of favor, but most forms of therapy use it to some extent. And, as we shall see, his theory of civilization is deeply flawed as he got the causal relationship between society and individuals backwards.

Freud's major mistakes, though, were in his general reasoning. The two biggest mistakes he made were generalizing too quickly from limited data and thinking that the specific patterns he saw in his culture were universal. Thus many of the specific symptoms he treated successfully were products of his culture and did not necessarily translate to other cultures or time periods.

The three most important things he got right, which impact on this work are the unconscious, the importance of sexuality in forming our sense of self, and his three-part view of what it is to be a person. We are, following Darwin, biological beings, then we become socialized. and finally we develop a sense of ourselves.

The unconscious is defined in terms of latent conceptions and memory. It is dynamic because unconscious ideas have an effect on us and/or can become conscious. It is the active unconscious that is revealed by the process of psychoanalysis.

> Unconsciousness is a regular and inevitable phase in the processes constituting our mental activity; every mental act begins as an unconscious one, and it may either remain so or go on developing into consciousness, according as it meets resistance or not.[6]

It can take a long time for psychoanalysis to break down these resistances. Another way to make this point is that even if we exhibit neurotic symptoms, our psyche sees our behavior as normal and any attempt to change as hostile.

The postulation of the unconscious is justified from clinical evidence and,

> Because the data of consciousness are exceedingly defective; both in healthy and in sick persons mental acts are often in process which can be explained only by presupposing other acts, of which consciousness yields no evidence.[7]

We are products of sexual—biological—reproduction. We inherit various characteristics, both physical and psychological. Of course, the nature/nurture debate will go on forever, but no one denies that both nature and nurture are factors in determining who and what we are. And because we are biological beings, and sexuality is a primary aspect of biology, sexuality plays a major role in determining not only how we see ourselves, but in how we organize our societies.

Briefly, in Freud's view of persons, we are born with a biological inheritance that includes basic survival drives and needs, as well as aspects of what our personalities will become. We are born into a social unit, such as a family or a clan, then we become socialized. As we learn how to behave in that social context we are taught what we can and cannot do. Then as we mature we run into conflicts between what we want and what our society says we cannot have. Out of this conflict we start devising ways to attain something of what we want. Thus we have our biological selves, our socialized selves, and our sense of personal identity.

The important points here have to do with the interaction between ourselves and our society, especially since so much of our identities are part of how we have been socialized.

We now have to understand how communities form and how cultures develop. Marvin Harris is an anthropologist greatly influenced by Freud even though he acknowledges that Freud got things both wrong and sometimes backwards. Freud began with the individual and tried to show how individual psychology led to the formation of culture. Harris argues that Freud got this backwards, since we are born into a culture we have to explain how the culture leads to the development of individual psychology.

Harris calls himself a cultural materialist, meaning that cultures can be studied in the same way that physical entities can be studied. There are causes and effects in terms of how cultures develop and how one cultural form leads to another. Thus,

> I think there is an intelligible process that governs the maintenance of common cultural forms, initiates changes, and determines their transformations along parallel or divergent paths. The heart of this process is the tendency to intensify production.[8]

Harris sees increased food production as a response to various threats to a culture, such as changes in climate, people migrations and competition for resources. He goes on to argue that such intensifications may be initially successful but always end up being counterproductive since "it leads to the depletion of the environment and the lowering of the efficiency of production."[9] Since this has always been the result, Harris wants to know why people always choose this approach. Clearly there are parallels to today's world, but this process started at the dawn of history. Why does it still persist?

The main theme of Harris' book is that cultures form as a result of the forms of life people take to insure their physical survival in their respective environments. Thus cultures can take many forms, depending on the nature of those environments. We cannot expect a people living near the Arctic Circle to develop a culture similar to people living near the equator. The ultimate question becomes which forms of life are needed to ensure survival, with food sources being a primary concern. Harris sees the main problem as balancing the population with food supply.

Most early cultures were hunter-gatherers, or, as Harris prefers to call them, gatherer-hunters, since most of their food came from gathering. But soon agriculture developed. Like many anthropologists Harris does not see agriculture as a step forward. The gatherer-hunter lifestyle was more advantageous in terms of securing a food supply and having to work a lot less for that food. As he states, "The idea of agriculture is useless when you can get all the meat and vegetables you want for a few hours of hunting and collecting per week."[10]

Why people turn to agriculture has to do with how they perceive their situations regarding food supply and population growth. When cultures compete for food they go to war. This was the case for gatherer-hunters as well as for farmers, but gatherer-hunter wars were not as vicious as warfare between agricultural communities for a number of reasons. First, agricultural communities were larger, and second, they were often permanent leading to permanent defenses. But Harris wants to know if the balance between populations and food supply is the social or political cause of war and why individuals are capable of warfare.

Following Ashley Montague Harris argues that "there are no drives or instincts or predispositions in human beings to kill other human beings on the battlefield, although under certain conditions they can easily be taught to do so."[11] So why do we do so? Harris sees the answer in terms of fertility and population growth. If populations could be controlled, or if there were always enough food to go around, even if there were competing peoples, conflicts would not occur. Harris sees the issue in terms of overpopulation, and in turn he sees the population question in terms of there being too many women who are giving birth: "The number of women determines the rate of fertility."[12] Thus, in times of war due to overpopulation, or at least due to not enough food to feed the existing population, women become devalued and a strong patriarchal society develops. This leads to such behaviors as female infanticide, since the group needs more defenders and fewer people. Thus,

> Without reproductive pressure neither warfare nor female infanticide would have become widespread and that the conjunction of the two represents a savage but uniquely effective solution to the Malthusian dilemma.[13]

The Malthusian dilemma, of course, is that Malthus saw populations increasing geometrically while food supplies increased arithmetically, thereby eventually leading to starvation.

To return to the main point, Harris sees social and sexual roles as being dependent on the nature of the culture and its relationship to the physical environment, with the physical environment being the source of food. A good example of this is presented by anthropologist Patricia Draper who studied two groups of Kalahari Bushmen of the !Kung tribe, one of which stayed as gatherer-hunters and the other developed a sedentary agricultural community. Draper compared the ways jobs were divided along sexual lines in the two groups.

> Features of sedentary life that appear to be related to a decrease in women's autonomy and influence are: increasing rigidity in sex-typing of adult work; more permanent attachment of the individual to a particular place and group of people; dissimilar childhood socialization for boys and girls; decrease in the mobility of women as contrasted with men; changing nature of women's subsistence contribution; richer material inventory with implications for women's work; tendency for men to have greater access to and control over such important resources as domestic animals, knowledge of Bantu language and culture, wage work; male entrance into extra-village politics; settlement pattern; and increasing household privacy,[14]

While the gatherer-hunter society seems to be the least sexist society known.

> Features, which promote egalitarianism between the sexes include women's subsistence contribution and the control women retain over the food they have gathered: the requisites of foraging in the Kalahari which entail a similar degree of mobility for both sexes; the lack of rigidity in sex-typing of many adult activities, including domestic chores and aspects of child socialization; the cultural sanction against the physical expression of aggression; the small size; and the nature of the settlement pattern.[15]

One conclusion from this discussion, as many anthropologists have pointed out, is that the development of agriculture was one of the worst things that happened in human history. This is so for at least three reasons: one, agriculture was far more labor intensive than the gatherer-hunter life; two, the role of women was degraded from equality to second class citizens; and three, warfare became more intense.

This discussion brings us back to Freud's view of personhood and the relationship between the individual and culture. We know that Freud saw women in a secondary role, though he finally realized he was wrong about women but was trapped in his framework. I have always believed that the main reason Freud encouraged women to become psychoanalysts was to get the psychology of women correct. But Freud's one sex view of women, where he saw women as mirror images of men, was completely wrong.

Harris' view is that Freud has the causal arrow between the individual and culture backwards. He had the psychodynamics right, but the relationships wrong. Freud saw the relationship between sexual dynamics and warfare, but instead of the sexual dynamics leading to warfare, it was warfare that led to the sexual dynamics in question. The dynamic in question is the famous oedipal complex. This complex arises at the onset of puberty when boys realize their sexuality and see their mothers as objects of the opposite sex, and then see their fathers as rivals. If the child works through this and matures properly there is no complex. Freud saw how a person with an unresolved complex would take out aggressions on women or on others. But Harris, looking at this dynamic from an anthropological standpoint, sees that living in a state of warfare where women are devalued is what leads to this dynamic.

Harris sees biological evolution as the basis of human culture, but he sees how the development of culture led to a change in human nature. And he also sees how biology and culture interact. Biological evolution led to changes in human culture, but these changes then led to changes in how humans evolved, especially with regard to culture. Thus, an important implication here is that biology is not destiny, for we can change the cultural conditions that lead to such behaviors.

So, where are we? We have seen that humans are biological creatures but there is an interplay between biology and culture, and that interplay, in the context of physical environments, is a determinant of specific behaviors. The important point here is that the culture—the community—is the important unit. We are all members of a community and it is the structure of the community that largely determines how we think about the world, about moral issues, and about ourselves.

The implications for moral and political theory then are obvious. We must develop a theory of culture, of society, and of how people function in that culture to set up a proper moral and political structure. The only political theory that does the job is something called Communitarianism. There are many versions of communitarianism, and some are more rigid about the roles of individuality than others. But it is communitarianism that we now turn to.

A good definition of communitarianism comes from Markate Daly in her introduction to her textbook, *Communitarianism: A New Public Ethics*,

> Communitarianism is a new philosophy, even though communal relationships form the fabric of all human societies and community centered philosophy goes back at least to ancient Greece. Even the term Is a contemporary neologism. As

a political philosophy, its originality lies in its union of community values with the democratic values of personal freedom and equality; its ideal is a democratic community. Communitarianism is a postliberal philosophy in the sense that it could only have developed within a liberal tradition of established democratic practices, and in a liberal culture that had allowed community values to decline to the extent that a corrective seemed necessary. Communitarianism was proposed as just such a corrective; its purpose is to bring the welfare of communities into the center of political discourse by establishing in the public domain the values of communal associations.[16]

Community is composed of a limited set of people who are bound together in networks of relationships."[17]

We will look at the notion of postliberal shortly, but first let us continue with the discussion of communitarianism. A view which brings some of these ideas together is that of Will Kymlicka.

In his book *Contemporary Political Philosophy* he lists the major theories of the day: Utilitarianism, Liberal Equality, Libertarianism, Marxism, Communitarianism and Feminism. The first three all begin with the individual. This leaves communitarianism and feminism. While I don't agree with all that he says about these views, I will begin with his definitions and then develop a view of political philosophy which I think will work. I will conclude by arguing that a form of communitarianism, informed by both the methodology of science and certain aspects of feminism, is a natural law approach to political theory.

Kymlicka begins his discussion of communitarianism by referring to the work of Michael J. Sandel, who defends a version of communitarianism, and defines communitarianism as a view that abandons the notion of the neutral state as seen in most forms of liberalism for a,

> Politics of the common good, where unlike the liberal individualistic conception of the common good—as seen in the quote from Bentham—In a communitarian society, however, the common good is conceived of as a substantive conception of the good life which defines the community's way of life.[18]

Examples of this notion of community can be found in the structure of a family, where we find we have certain commitments to others by the nature of being a member of that family. Since we do not choose to be a member of that family, and because those ties are not made by conscious decisions, they remain a part of us.

Kymlicka continues,

> This common good, rather than adjusting itself to the pattern of people's preferences, provides a standard by which those preferences are evaluated. The community's way of life forms the basis for public ranking of conceptions of the

good, and the weight given to an individual's preferences depends on how much she conforms or contributes to the common good.[19]

Kymlicka goes on to develop the notion of the "unencumbered self" where individuals "are free to question their participation in existing social practices, and opt out of them, should those practices seem no longer worth pursuing."

This is coupled with the notion of self-determination, both in social and economic matters. Kymlicka argues that communitarians see this view of the self as false. Thus he ends up rejecting communitarianism. He strengthens his position by showing that individualistic forms of political theory do not deny the notion of the common good. Thus, since individualistic theories maintain a conception of the common good and allow for self-determination, they are superior to communitarian views.

Clearly, I disagree with Kymlicka's conclusion regarding communitarianism and the notion of self-determination. But before getting into that discussion we must look at the notions of "liberal" and "postliberal" as that discussion will set up the rest of my argument.

Liberal is derived from the same Latin root as the word liberty, and a liberal democracy is one where individual liberty is prized and where individual human rights are guaranteed in the society's constitution or political structures. Liberal democracies also usually have some form of free market economy, since, at least from the work of Locke, free markets, free speech, and free assembly have all been associated together.

Post liberalism is, in part, a rejection of the excesses of the liberal order and the rejection comes from all sides. For example, the left criticizes how the multinational corporations seem to be controlling both the economy and the political agenda thereby subverting democracy. Thus articles appear in various media outlets talking about how democracies such as the United States have become oligarchies. While on the right, people feel as if they have been left out of the economy and revert to populism.

One could argue that most people are opposed to what is going on in the world today, but, given their different outlooks on life, they react differently. However, I wonder if, in a large sense, both sides would agree that going back to a more rational way of doing things, such as in the 1950s and 1960s, would satisfy their concerns. But then we would have to look at the myths versus the realities of that time period as well when it comes to arriving at specific conclusions as to how to restore the kind of social contract that existed back then.

As Stephen S. Cohen and J. Bradford DeLong argue,

> In 1944, with the end of the war in sight, the government was worried about how sixteen million returning GIs would find jobs. It passed the GI Bill, providing in place of a traditional veteran's bonus a generous program of support for

GIs wishing to go to college, plus a major mortgage assistance program with the valuable extra kicker of a possibly zero down payment. FHA insurance, the guarantor of the American dream, and with it the quasi-totality of government housing policy, was focused intensely on free-standing single-family homes.[20]

Then came the National Defense Highway Act which called for forty-one thousand miles of high-speed highways, with government paying ninety percent of the cost. Most of the highways were built for the newly developing suburbs.

The result of all this was,

> In the great migration to the suburbs, all but the poorest ranks of American families found their place and felt it to be the same place; middle-class America. Social scientists had difficulty understanding how and why a hefty majority of Americans persisted in saying that they were middle-class. Americans happily marched, or rather drove, out to take possession of their new suburban homes. Admittedly some houses were bigger and better than others; they had bigger lawns and bigger rooms and, crucially, they were surrounded by similar bigger houses. The progression of status and wealth signaled by the differentiation of suburbs was finely calibrated and well understood. . . . But the hierarchy of status and wealth did not delineate separate worlds. There were no "two nations." There was one nation—middle-class America—with some having more and better of the same thing.[21]

Thus the period from the 1940s through the 1970s saw a strong role by government to insure that people were able to participate in their communities. So a person driving a Chevy and a person driving a Cadillac both saw themselves as middle class because they both lived in the suburbs, drove on the same roads, and watched the same television programs. So even though their incomes may have been different, the similarities were more important than the differences.

Of course not all was great back then. There was tremendous racism and sexism. But for the people who participated in the economy, things were good.

The 1980s, with the beginnings of deregulation and changing taxation, started the inequalities we see today. Under the Republican president Eisenhower, in the 1950s, the top corporate tax rate was ninety percent and it was this money that paid for the highways. With tax rates dropping and deregulation happening, greater differences began to develop and so the concept of "middle-class" started to change. This points out the important role the over–all community, through its government, in maintaining a functioning community.

With so many people opposed to what is going on, as Daly points out, one result is to develop a new sense of community and to develop a new political philosophy based on that concept. Looking at history, and looking at the world today, we see many different kinds of communities. And that is fine, since we have established that culture is the main determining factor in how communities develop. And we should expect no less. Physical environments, as a basis of culture, also get us to see things differently. My favorite example is a group of stars we call The Big Dipper. But what if you live in a society that has no dippers? For example, the Inuit in Northern Canada see the same stars that we do but draw their line across the top and they see the great caribou in the sky. And, as we shall see, these differences in environment, and differences in culture, lead to differences in values.

Looking at how we use the word "community" today we see a whole range of uses, such as the black community, the legal community, the philosophical community, and so on. We use the term in these ways because we see commonality in the people who belong to these groups. But, as the above quote suggests, we rarely if ever these days talk about, say, neighborhoods as communities. We rarely if ever talk about communities in the physical sense. I think that is because we have largely forgotten about living in communities and now live and think as individuals, or as family members. But we rarely think of our neighbors as being members of our community, especially if we hardly know them, or see them as different from us. We may identify with our nations,—for example, I am American, or I am Canadian, or I am French. We may also identify with smaller regions such as states or provinces, or even sections of those areas. For example, I might think of myself as Canadian, but also as Southern Ontarian, for Northern Ontario has a very different culture. And we certainly identify with our families, even they are extended both in terms of many generations, many marriages or divorces and remarriages, or even over large distances.

What the individualism of liberalism has done is, as the above quote suggests, is to do away with a real sense of community. And this sets up a dichotomy between individuals and their communities. Which in turn "implies a contrast between two conceptions of the self; one grounded in community membership and the other in individual autonomy."[22]

One of the main implications of Lockean social contract theory is to show that in order to have rights and to function with other individuals we must become members of a community. To put this another way, from a political standpoint one cannot be a truly free individual unless one becomes a member of a community where all individuals provide mutual protection for each other.

When we look at current work in anthropology and linguistics we see that the view of the primacy of the community or culture over the individual is well supported. We are not born in isolation but into a community with a culture, a way of life, and a language which reflects that way of life. We are taught how to live in our culture and we learn the language socially. That language is used not only to report what we see and think and feel, but it also embodies a set of concepts which help to define the culture and the ways in which speakers of that language view the world.

Language develops both to communicate concerns and to educate future generations. We learn words like "table" and "chair" by coming into contact with these objects and by hearing people utter these sounds. But when we learn terms like "table" and "chair" we are not just learning specific terms, we are forming concepts. We learn to recognize a variety of objects as tables and chairs. As Wilfrid Sellars argues, nouns are singular distributive terms. They are singular because they refer to specific objects. They are distributive because they refer to a whole class of objects.

We learn our value language exactly the same way. Terms like "good" and "bad" are *not* subjective reaction or emotive words. They are substantive reporting distributive singular terms in the same way 'table' and 'chair' are. We *know* what is good and bad, even if we do not always act in accordance with that knowledge. In my book *Art Matters*, I argue for a distinction between "I like it" and "it is good." I can look at a painting, or a TV show, or read a book and say that I like it but I also know it is not good. Or, I can say I don't like something and acknowledge it is good. One is a personal reaction, the other is a critical evaluation. Thus the separation of fact from value is one of the worst things that has happened in the modern era since it takes away the cultural force of our values and reduces them to subjective feelings. It all began with David Hume who argued that "Reason is, and ought only to be the slave of the passions, and can pretend to no other office than to serve and obey them." Then, within a generation, we see Bentham arguing that "The community is a fictitious body, composed of individual persons who are considered as it were its members. The interest of the community then, is what?—the sum of the interests of the several members who compose it." He then goes on to argue that "it is vain to talk of the interest of the community without understanding what is in the interest of the individual."

Bentham's comments were made to support the moral aspects of the marketplace. Recall, Adam Smith saw the market as a moral system as long as people used their moral sensibilities. But then, as now, the market does not work because people do not use their sensibilities.

Another way of putting this point is to use Karl Polanyi's notion of "embeddedness." Through most of our history economics was embedded in our culture. But economics became divorced from culture in the 18th century. Instead of looking at economic theory as an aspect of culture, it became an abstract subject on its own, and much of cultural and political life became subservient to economic theory, all too often to the detriment of the overall society.

Now, Polanyi's main point is that for most of human history economic factors were embodied in a system where economics was not separated from other aspects of social and political life. What we know today as the free self-regulating market began to develop at the end of the eighteenth century, as has been chronicled by Adam Smith, but by 1815 the great transformation of Polanyi's title was complete,[23] and this new market economy transformed how people thought about the organization of society. In turn, it was this new thinking that led to conflicts between what marketeers thought was needed and what people affected by these changes needed. Thus, this free market is ultimately incompatible with democracy since people, through their political institutions and states, will want things that conflict with the workings of the market. In this context, Polanyi goes on to argue that the rise of fascism and communism at the end of the first world war and the beginning of the second world war were direct results of the failure of the market system.

> ... the origins of the cataclysm lay in the utopian endeavor of economic liberalism to set up a self-regulating market system. Such a thesis seems to invest that system with almost mythical faculties; it implies no less that the balance of power, the gold standard, and the liberal state, these fundamentals of the civilization of the nineteenth century, were, in the last resort, shaped in one common matrix, the self-regulating market.[24]

The background to this quote is that economic activity prior to this point in history had been "submerged in man's social relationships"[25] and that the two main principles of *"reciprocity* and *redistribution"*[26] provided the basis for the interaction of social, political, and economic life. But with the development of the market system the organization of society became transformed. "Instead of economy being embedded in social relations, social relations are embedded in the economic system. . . .This is the meaning of the familiar assertion that a market economy can function only in a market society."[27] And this market society becomes fragmented because a "self-regulating market demands nothing less than the institutional separation of society into an economic and a political sphere." It is this separation that leads to the commodification of everything from products to labor."[28] This commodification has dire consequences:

> To allow the market mechanism to be sole director of the fate of human beings and their natural environment indeed, even of the amount and use of purchasing power, would result in the demolition of society. For the alleged commodity "Labor power cannot be shoved about, used indiscriminately, or even left

unused, without affecting also the individual who happens to be the bearer of this peculiar commodity."[29]

The breakdown of this system in the 1930s led to the development of both socialism and fascism, opposite sides of the same coin. That the market system broke down should come as no surprise because of its utopian nature. The main point here is that,

> There was nothing natural about laissez-faire; free markets could never have come into being merely by allowing things to take their course. Just as cotton manufactures, the leading free trade industry were created by the help of protective tariffs, export bounties and indirect wage subsidies, laissez-faire was enforced by the state.[30]

Polanyi wrote this in 1944. One can only wonder at what he would have to say about the attempts to develop free trade today. The whole enterprise is based on a false premise and cannot work. But even Adam Smith knew that. Reading Smith's *The Wealth of Nations* as a follow-up to his earlier *Theory of Moral Sentiments* one can see that the market economy will only work if marketeers are concerned about the consequences of their actions on others, for Smith saw the workings of the market in moral terms. Smith's "invisible hand" was not just a self-regulating mechanism but a moral prescription.

As Karl Polanyi demonstrates in *The Great Transformation*, the notion of the market economy took the economy out of the culture and turned everything, including people, into a commodity. What happened in the seventeenth and eighteenth centuries, as is happening today, was a great increase in wealth along with a great increase in poverty. The people who were able to participate in the market got richer and the people who did not or could not participate in the market got poorer. Clearly the market does not work. For examples of this, just think of the homelessness and the use of foodbanks today. As the great Canadian political scientist of a century ago Stephen Leacock argued that the state is necessary for that purpose.[31]

Leacock recognizes that capitalism may be the best way to create wealth but acknowledges that laissez-faire capitalism cannot provide proper social services and good working conditions or control the use of child labor. For such concerns we need a democratic government, where the "good government" provides peace and order, to use the Canadian motto. How the government functions in the economy, of course, depends on the nature of the community it serves. Recall our argument about how communities have obligations to its members. So capitalism must be regulated to ensure that communities meet their respective moral obligations.

Another failing of the free market is nicely portrayed by John Kenneth Galbraith in his *A Short History of Financial Euphoria*. He shows that every time in history that the market was freed there was a boom and then a bust, from the great tulip craze of the 1600s to the market crash of 1929. And if the book had been written more recently, I am sure the crash of 2008 would also have been included. Galbraith's main point is that if economics were taught historically instead of ideologically economists would know that the unfettered market does not work.

Another point needs to be made here. In his influential book, *Economics as Moral Theory*, Bernard Hodgson demonstrates that economics is based on several assumptions regarding how people behave. He then shows how economists ignore negative evidence, thereby making economics a moral science instead of a natural science, to use eighteenth century terminology.

In a different context, 2019 Nobel Prize winners in Economics Abhijit V. Banerjee and Esther Duflo develop this theme. They begin by stating at the outset that they do not believe that when economists and the public have differing views the economists are always right. "We, the economists, are often too wrapped up in our models and our methods and sometimes forget where science ends and ideology begins."[32]

One example applies the so-called rule of supply and demand to immigration. They begin by stating that "(T)here is an important reason why facts are ignored, and it is based on a piece of economics seemingly so self-evident that many find it impossible to think past it, even when the evidence says the opposite."[33]

The standard argument, they state, is that the world is full of poor people who would earn more if they could find their way to a better, richer country. Then given a chance they would migrate. Standard economists then argue that this influx of poor people would drive down wages.[34] But as they point out, "The logic is simple, seductive, and wrong." This is so for two reasons. First, wage differentiations between countries have little to do with why people migrate. While there are people who are desperate to leave, the real question is why so many others don't move. And second, "there is no credible evidence that even relatively large inflows of low-skilled migrants hurt the local population.... Very little about it fits the standard story of supply and demand."[35]

A second standard view in economics is that workers would move to where the jobs are. The view assumes that wages do not depend on the worker's region or sector, but on what they bring to the table. "This is because the steelworker in Pennsylvania who loses his job because of foreign competition should move immediately to wherever he can find a job, to Montana or Missouri, to plating fish or making fisher-plates. After brief transitions, all workers with the same skills will earn the same."[36]

But, as Banerjee and Duflo point out, this does not happen. They call labor markets, "sticky." As was seen with migration, workers do not move even when market condition would appear that they ought to, thus wages are not equalized.[37]

But before continuing with an understanding of what a community is and how community politics can function, I want to look at an extreme form of individualism, known as libertarianism. This is a form of politics where governments are looked upon with suspicion and everything turns on individual action. Libertarianism is often associated with some form of market economy, since economics plays a large role in how libertarians see themselves in the world. So on to a look at libertarianism.

Libertarianism developed in a specific time and place and must be understood in that context. It could perhaps be seen as the antithesis of the medieval world's bureaucratic top down institutions of church and monarchy, where the individual counted for little, if anything. Thus emphasis on new-found freedom stressed the importance of the individual over the church or the state. It is in this context that we understand how capitalism and Protestantism developed together, as Max Weber has explained from a sociological standpoint.

But even when first properly formulated, individualistic approaches to moral theory were not as individualistic as writers today would have us believe. As we have seen, John Locke, who could be considered the grandparent of libertarianism, was concerned that as a result of the scientific revolution and its technological consequence, the industrial revolution, people left the land and the agrarian communities that the Catholic Church represented and moved to cities where they led more individualistic lives supported by Protestantism. With this development of industry also came more international trade and the development of the modern nation state. Locke tried to find an individualistic foundation for the state. He found it in the concept of the social contract,

> The state of nature has a law of nature to govern it. which obliges everyone, and reason, which is the law, teaches all mankind...that being all equal and independent, no one ought to harm another in his life, health, liberty or possessions.[38]

And this law of nature,

> would . . . be in vain if there were nobody that in the state of nature had a power to execute that law, and thereby preserve the innocent and restrain offenders. . . . And thus, in the state of nature, one man comes by a power over another; but yet no absolute or arbitrary power.

And this balance of power or contract works because,

> men living together according to reason without a common superior on earth, with authority to judge them, are properly in the state of nature.[39]

Thus, people in a state of nature—in their natural state—are free, and everyone is equal to everyone else. The social contract is an acknowledgment of this state of nature, this natural order of things. It is this natural freedom coupled with the human ability of rationality that provides the foundation of the social contract, which is just an acknowledgment of humanity's place in the natural order.

In a state of nature people must work to survive. This state of nature is not the Garden of Eden but Europe at the beginning of the industrial revolution. People require food and shelter. So people either work the land or build things. Working the land gives people privileges over the land and gives title to the land. This process, in turn, leads to the concept of private possessions. The organization around working and defending property heralds the beginnings of modern society. And this is where the notion of individual rights comes in. By working the land I now have a right to keep what I produce by my labor on the land. I have a right to defend my property and my person. Indeed, this is where the British slogan LIFE, LIBERTY AND THE PURSUIT OF PROPERTY comes from. This is the slogan that became LIFE, LIBERTY AND THE PURSUIT OF HAPPINESS in the American colonies, but became PEACE, ORDER AND GOOD GOVERNMENT in Canada.

One of the important aspects of individualism at this time was the notion that a person can have an identity independent of his or her community. For most of human history people identified with their community or tribe and so many of our names reflect this: the prefixes Mc, Mac, Ben, and so on all mean "son of" or "of the tribe of." But with the coming of the modern era and with people leaving the land, this identification changed. A good place to see this is in the novel *Robinson Crusoe* by Daniel Defoe. This book is usually considered the first true novel in that it was the first fictional narrative written in the first person where the reader did not know the ending, hence the name "novel." Crusoe maintains his personal identity while on the island. He creates an environment as close to what he came from, given the available materials, and his meeting with Friday, who does not have the Christian concept of God, illustrates Locke's views against innate ideas. The interaction between Crusoe and Friday also illustrates an example of a social contract. In short, the book is the world according to John Locke. Of course, we know today that anyone stranded on an island for that length of time would have gone insane. But in the early eighteenth century the belief in reason and this newfound identity made the story believable.

A century later Adam Smith develops Lockean philosophy in two directions. On the one hand Smith talks about the community and how individuals develop concerns for others through the development of the notion of sympathy. Following David Hume, Smith acknowledges "that one person cannot feel the pains of another, but we can judge another person's misfortunes through a comparison to our own pains by changing places in fancy with the sufferer, that we come either to conceive or be affected by what he feels." And when trying to understand another person's viewpoint Smith argues that "(T)o approve of another man's opinions is to adopt those opinions, and to adopt them is to approve of them."

Now, in his other work, *The Wealth of Nations*, Smith argues that we act from the standpoint of self-interest. Smith acknowledges that people act in social contexts and that,

> man has almost constant occasion for the help of his brethren, and it is in vain for him to expect it from their benevolence only. He will be more likely to prevail if he can interest their self-love in his favor and show them that it is for their own advantage to do for him what he requires of them.[40]

Thus even though we are alone in a state of nature, the correct use of reason will create a self-regulating system. While Smith does not refer to the *Sentiments* in *The Wealth of Nations*, in his day everyone would know that one could not read the latter book without having read the former.

Today, people tend to read *The Wealth of Nations* alone and do not see the influence of the *Sentiments* in the later work. But, as Robert Heilbroner points out, in his introduction to Smith's *work, both books reflect Smith's concerns with "social order and economic movement. . ."* The Sentiments deals with "the socialization of behavior" while *Wealth* develops this idea in the context of seeing how "the trajectory of a society of natural liberty"[41]) develops. My point is that to properly understand the notion of the invisible hand in *Wealth*, one must first understand the moral sense developed in the Sentiments.

But the tradition following David Hume undermined this sense of self-regulation and emphasized the importance of the individual. The major point can be seen in Hume's famous point: "Reason is, and ought only to be the slave of the passions, and can pretend to no other office than to serve and obey them."[42] Thus, within a generation, we see Bentham arguing that "The community is a fictitious *body*, composed of individual persons who are considered as it were its *members*. The interest of the community then, is what?—the sum of the interests of the several members who compose it." He then goes on to argue that "It is vain to talk of the interest of the community, without understanding what is the interest of the individual."[43]

So within 125 years of writing, Locke's views have been modified to the point that the whole notion of community becomes undermined. The individual prevails. And, as I shall argue, the whole moral basis of individualism also becomes undermined. The argument parallels the notion of individual pain and sensation discussed above. By stressing individuality over any sense of community the whole notion of sympathy, as Smith put it, becomes undermined, so that self-interested individuals cannot or need not concern themselves with other people. The irony here, though, is that the moral theory developed by these individualists was a consequentialist theory in which a person's actions were judged by how those actions affected other people.

The main point here is that Hume separated fact from value. Before Hume, all moral theorizing was done in what can be called a natural law context in which values were derived from an understanding of how the world works, the natural order of things, what persons are, and how persons fit into the way the world works. Natural law theory can be theological, as with Aquinas, or secular, as with Aristotle and Locke. But in all cases values—the nature of good and evil, the nature of right and wrong—were *known*. But with the development of individualism in the context of empiricism, values became, in the language of the twentieth century Humeans, expressions of emotion. That is why reason becomes subjugated to the passions when it comes to values; values are expressions of the passions.

Values become individualized. And while all persons can formulate their own views and follow their own passions, by separating fact from value, by divorcing people from their communities, we find two results for moral theory. The first is that each person must function in a value vacuum and determine his or her own values. Thus one person's subjective feeling becomes the basis for that person's actions. And this becomes the case for everyone. Any sense of evaluation becomes undermined since each person presents his or her view as THE view so no impersonal means of evaluation can be applied. My subjective sense determines what is right for me, as everyone else's subjective sense determines what is right for them. There can be no objective grounds to evaluate competing claims, except in terms of the consequences to others as spelled out in the social contract. We learn to equate "I like it" with "it is good."

The second point then, in Bentham's language, is to learn to maximize our interests. The second result is that in maximizing our own values, we no longer think of other people as our moral equals, but as obstacles on the road to our maximization.

We are now in a game which requires winners and losers. Of course, my actions have consequences and I can be punished for breaking the rules of the game. So I cannot outright steal from my competitors, nor can I eliminate them from the game. But, on this view, I do not have to regard them as moral equals, just as competitors, and as such I can treat them as means to an end, and not just ends in themselves. For example, say I am a corporate executive and want to maximize my profit. One way to do this is to lay off workers. Now, given the emphasis on the individual, it is up to these laid off workers to find their own new jobs. If they cannot, it is their fault. I no longer have any responsibility for them. And if they cannot find jobs, let them use their entrepreneurial skills and start their own businesses. That is what happens when we put the emphasis on the individual. And this practice, of course, is the basis for Marx' critique of capitalism, where he saw worker alienation and exploitation as the consequences of a social system that did not treat persons as moral equals.

A more contemporary critique of this practice can be found in *Surplus Powerlessness* by Michael Lerner. The argument of this book is that in most aspects of our lives we are not in control. How we must act is largely determined by social structures and any decisions we make are limited. Thus, in many aspects of our lives we are in fact powerless to change things. The notion of surplus powerlessness enters the picture when in fact I am powerless but am told I am responsible. So I blame myself for something over which I have no control. People in positions of power who use this argument against the laid off worker create surplus power by deflecting the responsibility from those who have power to those who do not.

Extreme individualism or libertarianism leads to a social order where people do not have to treat others morally—as moral equals—and can even deflect responsibility, thereby creating more moral inequality. Thus extreme individualism or libertarianism is at best amoral when it allows for manipulation, and at worst immoral when it allows for the exploitation of others while deflecting responsibility.

Now to return to my discussion of communitarianism and Kymlicka.

Clearly, I disagree with Kymlicka on the notion of self-determination. My argument takes two tracks. First, as I have already indicated, the whole conception of individuality is a function of community. Thus, the liberal view of individualism is false. Individuals are only as autonomous as their concepts of autonomy permit them to be. But these concepts come from the culture or are imbedded in the culture.

In a society which extolls extreme individualism, especially coupled with a capitalist mentality which allows for all persons to maximize their profits, it becomes easy for individuals to opt out of the notion of social responsibility and simply claim that they are following the rules of their society which says that they are allowed to take advantage of others if others are capable of being taken advantage of.

Clearly this turns common notions of utilitarianism and Kantian morality on their heads, but certainly appears to be at the basis of a great deal of economic activity in capitalist or corporate contexts.

My second track is to argue that self-determination and the ability to opt out of various social practices are NOT incompatible with communitarianism. The argument will have numerous side trips but will eventually get back on the main track. The first side trip is to revisit individualism just to reiterate that any concept of individualism is derived from the language of the culture. As individualism developed in the seventeenth century onward it kept evolving to a point where the concept of the individual seemed to exist independently of any culture and, conversely, culture became understood as a group of individuals. But, since all individuals shared this view, and also shared the same language and value concepts, we see that individuals never completely leave their culture behind.

Perhaps the strongest view regarding individualism comes from the combined views of novelist/philosopher Ayn Rand and self-actualization psychologist Abraham Maslow.[44] It should come as no surprise that they had a mutual admiration for each other's work. Maslow's view of human psychology states that we go through stages to become self-actualized. Rand argued that the self is the most important aspect of life. To refer to her major novel, if Atlas were holding the world and if he were hurt, he should shrug and save himself. This is consistent with Maslow's self-actualized individual for this individual needs no one else. Such people are psychologically self-sufficient. They are morally autonomous individuals who do not refer to other people when acting. Selfishness becomes the number one virtue. And, if pushed to an extreme, because of their apparent autonomy and separation from culture, such individuals can be seen as amoral since they act outside cultural norms. And, since we know that Maslow was highly influenced by Nietzsche, we can portray Maslow's self-actualized person as a kind of Nietzschean amoral superman.

Can we develop a concept of individuality which does not lead to the divorcing of the individual from the social context? Happily, the answer is yes. Such a conception comes from feminist theory which emphasizes the notion of "connectedness." This involves recognizing that while people are autonomous they are also part of a culture. In order to do so, the feminist movement in the 1970s realized that the Maslow model of self-actualization, which was seen as the way to go by early feminists in the 60s, did not work because of social structures. The issue is often discussed in terms of systemic belief systems. Because of the ways we learn our values, we usually do not challenge them and are often put in confusing situations when confronted with something new. A story that was popular in the 60s and through the 80s and 90s clearly exhibits this. A boy and his father go for a drive. They are in a crash. The father is killed, and the boy is rushed to hospital. Upon entering the operating room, the doctor looks at the boy and says, "I can't operate on him. That is my son." What is the relationship between the doctor and the boy?

All kinds of answers were proffered from the doctor being the actual biological father, or the wife's first husband. The answer, of course, is that the doctor is the boy's mother. But since it was rare for women to be doctors, let alone surgeons, most people did not get it.

As a result of the failure of individualistic psychology, there was a return to psychoanalysis since that was the only theory of psychology with a social dimension. The important figure here is Nancy Chodorow whose work, as we have seen, includes the important distinction between sex and gender. In this context Jean Grimshaw argues that,

> The human self is "embedded" in a network of relationships with others, both at the very immediate and intimate and at wider levels. Human needs and interests arise in a context of relationships with other people, and human needs for relationships with other people cannot be understood as merely instrumental to isolate individual ends. For all these reasons, it is right to reject an "individualistic" account of the human self.[45]

The so-called ethics of care looks at the context of the behavior in question and at the relationships of the people involved in the situation so the context of the behavior can be understood, instead of taking abstract principles and applying them to a situation. Thus feminist ethics looks at social connections instead of abstract autonomy. And it is this social or community context which makes feminist theory in general, and the feminist concept of the self in particular, supportive of a communalist approach to politics.

The next track we are going to ride on is to look at the social context of science. As we have learned from historians and philosophers of science such as Thomas Kuhn and Wilfrid Sellars, science is a value-laden problem-solving enterprise. People have a problem. They investigate. Upon investigation they formulate hypotheses which they test. If the test bears out, they formulate a theory to explain how and why the particulars obey generalities (laws). Theories about different things are put together to form frameworks or paradigms. After a time new problems may arise, or as a result of the accumulated knowledge, questions are now asked that were never thought of before. So new investigations begin which may yield knowledge that does not fit in with our old knowledge. For example, the Aristotelian view of the world was maintained for close to two thousand years but was finally demonstrated to be false by the scientific revolution of the sixteenth and seventeenth centuries. Copernicus's and Galileo's views of the heliocentric view of the universe and

Newton's laws of motion, of optics, and of gravity, showed Aristotle's view of the earth centric universe to be false, along with his views on causality. But the relationship between Aristotle and Newton is not just one of true versus false. In showing Aristotle's view of the world to be false, Newton explained things differently. Thus the views are incommensurable. And current physical theory shows Newtonian theory to be false on the atomic level. Thus knowledge advances, not by adding to what we know but by transforming it.

The process of scientific change has been characterized by Sir Karl Popper as a continuous form of conjecture and refutation.[46] The important point here is that though science yields truth, truth is provisional; we may learn something tomorrow that will show what we know today to be false. Ideological thinking is anathema to science, as it should be for everything else. Ideological thinking, whether in religion, economics, or politics, closes us to new information. And new information can lead to the questioning of our old values as well. New knowledge ends up describing the world, and our relation to that world, differently, leading to new values, and creating a whole new framework or paradigm.

In a very real way, the process of science parallels democratic societies, where problems arise, and people present new ideas and new solutions. Thus, individual freedom is as necessary for the development of science as it is for the development of democracy.

To make a broader point, the process of science parallels what goes on the social realm. If it did not, we would still be living in some ancient social structure. The analogy between the scientific process and the social one is that in our communities, where we share basic views about the world, we also have differences, like scientists testing different hypotheses in an atmosphere of free and open debate. In science, in politics, in our communities, differences are debated openly, fostering not only the ideal of free speech but of tolerance for opposing views.

We are all members of a community. Probably, depending on how we function in the world, we are all members of a number of different, overlapping communities. We identify with our state or province, with our town, with our country, with our job, with our religion, with our ethnic backgrounds, and so on. We are also individuals with different views on things, but with a shared view of the overriding values of our community. We debate these differences and we are tolerant of opposing views. But we still acknowledge that we are members of the same community and that the community is bigger than the sum of the individuals in it. Constitutions and institutions exist beyond individuals, even if individuals can transform them. Thus individual liberties, questioning, and self-determination are completely compatible with communitarianism.

But what does it mean to have a communitarian system? Obviously, there can be many versions, as there are different forms of communities, but my understanding of communitarianism is that the community has responsibilities to its citizens, and, in turn, citizens have responsibilities to their community.

If we look back to anthropology, we always talk of community or culture. And, given my argument that one has to recognize one is a member of a community before one becomes an individual in a political sense, the community must make it possible for each member of the community to be able to function as an individual. Individuals must be educated with both the academic abilities and job skills needed to function. Individuals must be assured of their survival, so basic medical care must be provided to all members of the community. And if there is some notion of a free market economy operating, the community must ensure that wages are high enough so that people can afford basic commodities, and businesses must operate within cultural values. Another way of putting this point is to argue that how the economy functions is a factor of the culture, rather than having the economy determine how the culture works. Citizens must be well informed if they are going to make decisions which can affect the community as a whole. Thus knowledge must be at the base of moral decision-making.

NOTES

1. Darwin, Charles, *The Origin of Species*, (New York: Mentor, 1958) 122.
2. For a detailed discussion of these issues see Eva Jablonka and Marion J. Lamb, *Evolution in Four Dimensions: Genetic, Epigenetic, Behavioural, and Symbolic Variation in the History of Life.* Cambridge: (MIT Press, 2005).
3. Jacob, Francois, *The Logic of Life, A History of Heredity*, (New York: Vintage Books, 1976) 205.
4. Jacob, 208.
5. For a discussion of these issues see Eva Jablonka and Marion J. Lamb, *Evolution in Four Dimensions*.
6. Freud, "A Note on the Unconscious" in *General Psychological Theory*, ed by Phillip Rieff (New York: Collier Books, 1963) 53.
7. Freud, "The Unconscious" in, *General Psychological Theory* ed by Phillip Rieff, (New York: Collier Books, 1963) 116–117.
8. Harris, Marvin ,*Cannibals and Kings, The Origins of Culture*, (New York: Random House, 1987) 4.
9. Harris, 4.
10. Harris, 26.
11. Harris, 37.
12. Harris, 39.

13. Harris, 41.
14. Draper in Reiter, Patricia, "!Kung Women: Contrasts in Sexual Egalitarianism in Foraging and Sedentary Contexts" in *Towards and Anthropology of Women*, edited by Rayna Reiter,(New York: Monthly Review Press, 1975).
15. Draper in Reiter.
16. Markate Daly, ed. *Communitarianism: A New Public Ethics*, (Belmont: Wadsworth, 1993{xiii}).
17. Markate Daly, xv.
18. Kymlicka, Will, *Contemporary Political Philosophy: An Introduction* (Oxford: Clarendon Press, 1990) 91–92.
19. Kymlicka,
20. Cohen, Stephen J. and Bradford DeLong, *Concrete Economics: The Hamilton Approach to Economic Growth and Policy*, (Cambridge: Harvard Business Review Press, 2016).
21. Cohen and Delong, 92–93.
22. Daly, xvi.
23. Polanyi, Karl, *The Great Transformation: The Political and Economic origins or our Time*, (Boston, beacon Press, 2001) 7.
24. Polanyi, 31.
25. Polanyi, 48.
26. Polanyi, 49–50.
27. Polanyi, 60.
28. Polanyi ,74–75.
29. Polanyi, 76.
30. Polanyi, 145.
31. Leacock, Stephen, *Elements of Political Science*, (Boston: Houghton Mifflin,1921).
32. Banerjee Abhijit V. and Esther Duflo, Good Economics for Hard Times, (New York: Hard Times, 2019) 5.
33. Banjeree and Duflo, 12.
34. Banjeree and Duflo, 12.
35. Banjeree and Duflo, 13.
36. Banjeree and Duflo, 61.
37. Banjeree and Duflo, 62.
38. Locke, in Barker, 5.
39. Locke, 6.
40. Smith, Adam, *Theory of Moral Sentiments*, in Heilbroner, Robert L. ed, *The Essential Adam Smith* (New York: W.W. Norton & Company, 1987).
41. Smith, *Wealth of Nations*, 9 In Heilbroner.
42. Hume, David, *An Inquiry Concerning Human Understanding*, ed by L.A. Selby-Bigg, (Oxford, The Clarendon Press, 1967) 415.
43. Bentham, Jeremy, *An Introduction to the Principles of Morals and Legislation*, in Steven M. Cahn and Peter Markie, eds, *Ethics: History, Theory and Contemporary Issues* (New York: Oxford University Press, 1998) 319.

44. Ayn Rand is best known as a novelist. See her *Atlas Shrugged* for an approach to her selfish individualism See Maslow's *Toward a Psychology of Being* for his individualistic approach, along with his hierarchy of needs.

45. Gimshaw, Jean, *Philosophy and Feminist Thinking*, (Minneapolis: University of Minnesota Press, 1986).

46. Popper, Sir Karl, *Conjectures and Refutations*, (London: Routledge and Kegan Paul,) 1965 specially chapter 1.

Chapter Two

Multiculturism

I want to deal with multiculturism first for two reasons. The first is because part of my approach to ethical issues is from a cultural standpoint, and the second is that the issue overlaps a number of other issues and as such provides a good introduction to the book.

Multiculturism is primarily about how different cultures interact with each other. These interactions can take place in a variety of ways, with people living in the same vicinity holding different religious beliefs, holding different cultural beliefs, and speaking different languages.

Different societies, different countries, deal with these issues in different ways. In this chapter I will look at a number of different countries and how they deal with these issues. But first, let us properly follow the schema set out in the introduction and define our issues.

METAPHYSICS

In the case of multiculturism, the main issue is about how peoples of different views—cultural practices, ethical concepts, language, skin color—interact. What kinds of conflicts can arise, or have arisen, in such situations? How can such conflicts be resolved?

These issues all have to do with multiculturism in one society or country. Another issue has to do with different countries interacting with one another, especially when those different countries reflect very different values.

The argument in favor of multculturism is based on the notion of tolerance—that all people are equal and as such all views are equal—and therefore must be tolerated. Or, to put this point more strongly, other people must be accepted. The basic idea of multiculturism developed after the Second World

War in part as a reaction to the racism and genocide seen in that conflict. Thus, multiculturism is used to combat racism and to protect minority rights.

The main arguments against multiculturism have to do with protecting majority rights, and under the guise of multiculturism, negative practices may be allowed to flourish. One example of this is in societies where women have few, if any, rights; people opposed to multiculturism see the concept as allowing the denial of these rights in a society which has equal rights for women. On the opposite side, people have argued that because of multiculturalism, when people from such societies come to a society where there are women's rights, the rights of the newcomers are denied. Another argument against multiculturism is that it leads to ghettoization where people of like backgrounds live in enclaves and do not try to integrate since they are already seen as equals in their new homes. And this, in turn, can lead to further segregation.

A final argument against multicluturism comes from the Tower of Babel story in that people who accept this story literally believe the purpose of the destruction of the tower was to keep the different people separate.

EPISTEMOLOGY

Here we will look at specific cases. First we will look at the policies of different countries and see how they differ both in stated policies and in their effectiveness. We will look at how immigrants and refugees are regarded by their new host nations. Then we will look at more specific issues such as linguistic and racial conflicts. These latter issues can be found in existing societies as well as in societies with new immigrant populations.

I will start with Canada, which is famous for its multicultural policy. Here is an except from the official act:

(1) It is hereby declared to be the policy of the Government of Canada to

   (a) recognize and promote the understanding that multiculturalism reflects the cultural and racial diversity of Canadian society and acknowledges the freedom of all members of Canadian society to preserve, enhance and share their cultural heritage;
   (b) recognize and promote the understanding that multiculturalism is a fundamental characteristic of the Canadian heritage and identity and that it provides an invaluable resource in the shaping of Canada's future;
   (c) promote the full and equitable participation of individuals and communities of all origins in the continuing evolution and shaping of all aspects of Canadian society and assist them in the elimination of any barrier to that participation;

(d) recognize the existence of communities whose members share a common origin and their historic contribution to Canadian society, and enhance their development;
(e) ensure that all individuals receive equal treatment and equal protection under the law, while respecting and valuing their diversity;
(f) encourage and assist the social, cultural, economic and political institutions of Canada to be both respectful and inclusive of Canada's multicultural character;
(g) promote the understanding and creativity that arise from the interaction between individuals and communities of different origins;
(h) foster the recognition and appreciation of the diverse cultures of Canadian society and promote the reflection and the evolving expressions of those cultures;
(i) preserve and enhance the use of languages other than English and French, while strengthening the status and use of the official languages of Canada; and
(j) advance multiculturalism throughout Canada in harmony with the national commitment to the official languages of Canada.
(f) generally, carry on their activities in a manner that is sensitive and responsive to the multicultural reality of Canada.[1]

A large part of this policy has to do with Canada's origins as a bicultural country, with two founders, English and French. And, as some commentators add, a third founder in indigenous peoples has had an effect on the evolution of Canadian laws and customs. Thus, as can be seen, a consequence of Canada's policy is to see all peoples are seen as equals. One of the consequences of this approach to the issue is that Canada has what is known as "hyphenated Canadians"—people who immigrate to Canada are encouraged to maintain their heritage while adapting to Canada. So Canada has, for example, Haitian-Canadians, Salvadorian-Canadians, Syrian-Canadians, Somali-Canadians, and so on.

Three simple examples exhibit this. First A Sikh person, who must wear a turban, applied to be a member of the RCMP, Canada's national police force. He was rejected on the grounds that because of his turban he could not wear the proper uniform. When he challenged this, it was ruled that if Canada is to be truly multicultural, adaptations must be made. He can wear the full uniform and his turban.

Second, another Sikh applied for a motorcycle license and was denied on the grounds that he would not be able to wear the mandated helmet for safety reasons. That ruling was upheld.

A third example is the case of Muslim women who wear the niqab, a veil that covers the face leaving only the eyes visible. They can wear it but must be able to identify themselves when dealing with public institutions such as voting.

The point here is that Canada tries to acknowledge people's origins, religions and customs, but also shows that Canadian laws and customs must also be adhered to. Thus the over all effect is that Canada maintains real multiculturism while also maintaining its own laws and customs.

On the negative side, there is no strong incentive to completely assimilate. Yet, according to Statistics Canada from a 2013 survey of 7,003 immigrants who landed between 1980 and 2012 from 182 countries with diverse ethnic and racial backgrounds:[2]

The results show that 93 percent of immigrants had a very strong or a strong sense of belonging to Canada. Furthermore, a strong sense of belonging to the receiving country is not necessarily incompatible with a sense of belonging to the source country. About 69 percent of all immigrants had strong sense of belonging to both Canada and their source country (the integrated belonging profile). Another 24 percent of immigrants had a strong sense of belonging to Canada and a weak sense of belonging to their source country (the national belonging profile). In comparison, very few (three percent) had a strong sense of belonging to their source country but a weak sense of belonging to Canada (the source-country belonging profile); and very few (four percent) had a weak sense of belonging to both Canada and their source country (the weak belonging profile).

Now we turn to the United States.

The United States is known as a "melting pot" and as such has no official policy of multiculturism.

The United States makes no affirmation of multiculturalism, although the Department of Justice's Community Relations Service (CRS) does act as a "peacemaker" for community conflicts and tensions arising from differences of race, color, and national origin (United States Department of Justice 2010). The Department of Justice notes that the CRS, which was created by the Civil Rights Act of 1964, is "the only Federal agency dedicated to assist[ing] State and local units of government, private and public organizations, and community groups with preventing and resolving racial and ethnic tensions, incidents, and civil disorders, and in restoring racial stability and harmony." The CRS is not explicitly tasked with furthering or promoting multiculturalism but acts, in effect, as a conciliator among various cultural communities. Initially, Black-white relations were the focus, but this has shifted somewhat to also include relations between white and Arab and Muslim Americans.[3]

An issue not mentioned in this excerpt is the role of Spanish speakers in the United States. In many states Spanish is spoken regularly. We see signs in public places in Spanish, but unlike Canada where both French and English are official languages—Canada is officially bilingual—the United States does not recognize Spanish as an official language.

The issue of majority identity is a big problem in the United States. In a study of 26,200 people Harvard professor Robert D. Putnam found that in racially diverse communities there was a lack of trust in the leaders of the community. People don't trust the mayor, the newspaper and other institutions.

And next we look at The Netherlands.

While the notion of "pillarization" had historically been popular in the Netherlands—referring generally to elite cooperation among religious and ideological communities—it began to lose favour in the 1960s. While not explicitly replaced by a discourse of multiculturalism, the Minorities' Policy, which was passed in 1979, allowed for parallel institutional arrangements and could be considered "multiculturalist."

Such policies began to decline, however, with the focus shifting in the late 1990s to integration and assimilation. After the 1994 election, the Christian Democrats replaced the Dutch Minorities Policy with the Integration Policy. This shifted Dutch policy away from the recognition and maintenance of cultural diversity. The Integration Policy focused heavily on the socio-economic incorporation of immigrants. However, the introduction of the Integration Policy was not, at that point, a refutation of multiculturalism per se, but rather a reaction to unemployment, poor educational outcomes and social disadvantage among immigrants. The former Minorities Policy was criticized for not adequately addressing these challenges.[4]

- Since 1998, new immigrants have been required to take an integration course.
- Since 2003, naturalization has been conditional on passing a civics exam.
- In 2006, the Dutch Minister of Culture introduced a cultural Canon of the Netherlands.
- In 2007, the New Civic Integration Act broadened compulsory integration programs to all foreigners from outside of the European Union.
- Most assessments suggest hard-line assimilation policies were only readily apparent after the 2002 assassination of Pim Fortuyn, although certainly in the period between 1994 and 2002, there was some movement away form a multiculturalist orientation. While integration policies do retain some of the influences of multiculturalism—particularly at the local level—there is no explicit affirmation of multiculturalism nor any separate ministry or agency to implement the policy. While there are some ethnic advisory bodies, these are far less powerful than they were in the past.[5]

Dutch right-wing politician Pim Fortuyn, who led his anti-immigration party to a position of prominence in the Netherlands, was assassinated in 2002.[6]

In the Netherlands the main concern with multiculturism has to do with non-European cultures, which are negatively viewed. The assumption is that for a society to work it must be homogenous and that non-European cultures cannot assimilate.

And finally let us look at Germany.

When talking about Germany one must keep in mind the aftermath of the Second World War where Hitler tried to have a pure race and tried to exterminate all non-Aryans. Recall the Holocaust.

> Immigration to Germany has typically been a highly politicized issue. Although Germany has not traditionally positioned itself as an "immigration country," the 2005 election of a coalition government composed of the Christian Democratic Union and Social Democratic Party brought with it an increasing appetite to address the country's growing diversity. A new Immigration Act was passed in 2005, and there has been a move toward the creation of various integration policies. At the national level at least, there has, however, been a conscious effort not to label these "multiculturalism" policies.

In addition, in debates on integration, Germany treats immigrants with a regular residence status differently from those with a so-called "tolerated" status. Those with a regular residence status are encouraged to integrate, and there are initiatives to facilitate this; those with a tolerated status are explicitly encouraged not to integrate as the ultimate goal is to see them return to their country of origin.

Consultation with ethnic communities in the development of policies has been uneven. For example, although an Expert Council on Immigration and Integration was dissolved in 2005 following public outcry over its recommendation that labour immigration be increased, there are some more recent examples of Germany's efforts to involve civil society in the crafting of immigration and integration policies. An Integration Summit was convened in 2006, and it involved several migrant organizations. One catchphrase for the Summit was "talking to migrants, not about them."

The Federal Office for Migration and Refugees is the department chiefly responsible for immigration and ethnic communities. The government's primary legislative obligations with respect to immigrant integration are outlined in section 43 of the Residence Act (2004). It stipulates that integration is a joint responsibility of the immigrant and the state, that foreigners must learn enough about German life to live without assistance, and that a basic package of integration courses will be offered to facilitate this. The act also requires the government to develop an integration plan. In this vein, a National Integration Plan was released in 2007; in the months leading up to its development, the government actively engaged immigrant associations and communities. Nonetheless, some Turkish associations were upset about some of the proposed requirements, including those related to the language skills required by family migrants; they opted to boycott the summit.

In terms of the commitments made in the Integration Plan, some of these appear to be derived from multicultural principles but, again, multiculturalism is not explicitly mentioned. This is partly because. . . multiculturalism is viewed as an "easy-going relativism" that does not give the state a sufficient role in mediating between the culture of the host society and those of newcomers.

Instead, the government says that integration is a combination of "promoting and demanding." It "requires an effort from everyone, from government and society. Decisive is the migrants' willingness to get involved with life in our society, to unconditionally accept our Basic Law and our entire legal system and, in particular, to visibly demonstrate the belonging to Germany by learning the German language. On the side of the host society, acceptance, tolerance, civic commitment and willingness to honestly welcome people living lawfully among us, are essential. . . The diverse migrants' abilities have not been sufficiently acknowledged and promoted thus far. The Federal Government would like to change this in the future."

While the Integration Plan outlined responsibilities of the federal government, it also committed funds to municipal governments and NGOs so that they could deliver integration programs. As such, there is an important local dimension to integration. Some of these cities have been active on this front for some time. Frankfurt, for example, has had an Office for Multicultural Affairs since the 1980s; note, however, that this is the only city in Germany that uses the word "multiculturalism" to describe its approach. Stuttgart, meanwhile, developed a "Pact for Integration" in 2001 in collaboration with NGOs and civil society groups. It recognizes cultural diversity as a resource to be cultivated and lists peaceful cohabitation, social cohesion and the promotion of participation and equal opportunities for all residents among its goals (ibid.). Stuttgart also has a municipal Integration Department, which is advised by 13 members of city council and 12 community members with immigrant backgrounds. The city also publishes information in several languages and hosted a roundtable on religions in 2003. There is support for, and ongoing debate over, the adoption of multiculturalism at the municipal level.

The main problem that European countries have with immigration and refugees is that because they are, by and large, homogenous societies, they have difficulty in absorbing peoples of different backgrounds, so these migrants tend to end up living in isolated communities and do not get to participate in the larger society.

For example, in Germany there is a great discussion over the concept of *Heimat*, "which mixes the concepts of homeland with a sense of belonging." As Professor Hermann Bausinger of the University of Tubingen said, "Heimat is the product of a feeling of conformity with a person's own small world. When people are no longer secure in their surroundings, when they are constantly exposed to irritations, then that Heimat is destroyed."[7]

In Germany there seems to be a totally two-sided view. According to the article, most Muslims who have been in Germany feel they have assimilated, while Germans are concerned about seeing differences and are opposed to assimilation of people who are different and who would pose a threat to Heimat.

VALUES

Here we will look at the specific issues with regard to how to resolve them using the values set out in the preceding two chapters.

LOGIC

Finally, we will make connections between cultural practices in different contexts and apply values to see if solutions can be arrived at, as well as evaluating the reasons given for the various positions.

DISCUSSION

There are a number of reasons for the existence of multicultural societies. One is conquest and colonization. One culture or nation conquers another, moves in, and over time as the relationship changes, the two different cultures develop a means of coexistence. We see this all over the world, for example, the British in North America, the British in India, and the French, Germans, Spanish, and others in other parts of the world, notably Asia and Africa. A second reason for the existence of multicultural societies is immigration and refugees. Immigrants and refugees leave their homelands for different reasons, mainly by choice or by necessity, but the impact on their new homelands is similar. A third reason is globalization, where jobs, capital and people cross borders. This is especially the case in Europe.

Immigrants and refugees leave their homelands for different reasons, but the issues of dealing with them in their new lands are somewhat similar in that both groups have to learn to live in the new land. But the response from the new, or host, land is different because immigrants, primarily, are welcomed, while refugees are not so readily welcomed. However, in both cases, the new land has to learn to accept or at least accommodate the newcomers. First let us focus on immigrants. Then we can look at the specific issues regarding refugees.

When looking at the issue of immigration, we must look at both sides of the issue—the immigrant and the host country. Each side has to meet the other; each has obligations to the other.

When someone lands in a new country, they must learn something about their new home. They must learn something about basic laws and customs, about the political system, about the educational system, and about how the world of employment works.

And the host country, which has invited these immigrants, must make provisions so that people who come from very different backgrounds can learn to function in the host country. The country must provide basic necessities so that immigrants can adjust to their new lives. Access to education, second language learning, and trade instruction must be provided.

Also the host country must find ways to allow foreign credentials to be adapted so that trained professionals do not have to resort to unprofessional jobs.

Allowing for the isolation of immigrants does not do them any good, for being isolated means they will never be able to properly participate in their new country. And total assimilation is just as bad since it appears to put a low value on the traditions and home countries of the immigrants.

So immigration is a complex issue which must be looked at from both sides, and both sides must adapt to their new situations.

In looking at cross-cultural behaviors we have to look at how people understand their own culture and how they understand their new situation. We do this in two ways: First we look at how we define our respective practices, and second, we try to put ourselves on the receiving end of our actions to see if we would be prepared to accept the consequences of our own actions.

The first method involves making an important distinction between what is a necessary part of our practice and what is not. For example, let us look at what would happen if certain rules of games were changed. For those of you who understand baseball, you know the designated hitter rule has not changed the game. Whether or not the pitcher bats or not is not a necessary part of the game. If we allowed pinch runners but did not replace those players, the game would also not change very much. But if we did away with the foul tip rule on the third strike, we would see a tremendous change in the game. Thus the third strike rule is a necessary part of the game, as we understand it.

For those of you who follow formula one racing, think of the rule changes regarding safety. The early safety rules about having proper medical facilities at the track and having guardrails around the track did not change how people drove. But newer rules regarding smaller wings providing less downforce and treaded tires which slow down the cars have changed how cars are driven. It is much more difficult to overtake because of the reduced downforce. So the sport has changed. While no one wants to dispute the need for safety, what has happened is that in the push for safety the nature of the sport has been changed.

So we see how some changes in practices have little effect on the process and others have significant effects on the process.

If the process—the game, the cultural practice—has been changed significantly, the question becomes one of seeing if the changes were worthwhile. We do this by putting the person or persons who advocate the changes into the new situation. If I were an advocate of the change of the foul tip rule, and I played baseball and liked the game, how would I like the game if I had to play it without the foul tip rule? Would I still want to play? And if I liked to race, and knew we needed to update safety rules, but not to the point of seriously affecting the sport, would I still want to race after these rule changes?

In either case, if the answer is no, then I should not implement those changes.

This is how we test moral pronouncements. We see how the change in practice that is advocated by the new rules affects the practice, and as advocates of the changes, we put ourselves on the receiving end of the changes to see if we would want to live with them.

Above I mentioned three cases that Canadians have dealt with. But now let us look at the other side. What if Canadians moved to countries that required men to wear turbans and women to wear veils or other face coverings? Would Canadians or Americans, or even Europeans, accept such practices? Or would they decide not to participate in their new country's institutions or practices?

By raising the question this way we see the complexity of the issue. When looking at the issue from a different perspective we can try to come to some kind of accommodation. While women of this particular belief must be veiled in public would there be a situation in which they could lift the veil briefly to ensure proper identification and do it in a way that would not compromise their beliefs?

One possibility would be to have the woman raise her veil only to another woman and to do it with some kind of privacy. In this way the Canadian institution is maintained, the immigrant culture is maintained, and the immigrant can partake in a Canadian institution.

This positive outcome is achieved by both sides making adaptations and the adaptations can be made for two reasons: One is that both sides look at the other side to see what has to be done to participate in both traditions, and the second is to come to understand what is important from the other person's perspective.

In this way we can use principles of moral theory to arrive at cultural compromises which allow for the continuation of multiculturalism and cultural tolerance. And this process must be a two-way street. The immigrants must also learn to adapt their behaviors to learn to live in their new country.

To put this point another way, let us look at science as a problem-solving enterprise. We define a problem, we look the situation, with what we know, we formulate a hypothesis which leads us to investigate the situation further and, hopefully, come to a conclusion. With regard to immigration we formulate the problem of how we adapt to our new country and how the citizens of that country adapt to, or accept, immigrants.

Immigrants come to a new country for a variety of reasons. They are still proud of their heritage and try to maintain some of their customs in the new land. But they also have to adapt to the new country.

So we formulate a problem. What is the best way to live in this new country? We formulate three possible answers: (1) try to maintain as much of our homeland practices as we can; (2) completely abandon those practices and learn how to become a good citizen of our new country by adopting the practices of the new country; or (3) try to find some kind of compromise between maintaining some traditions and adopting new ones here.

We know that the first one will not work. If we never learn to adapt to our new surroundings we can never enter into any kind of life here. The second is a good idea but takes time. So we are left with the third option, even if we want to eventually end up with the second option.

So we go about learning as much as we can about our new country. We learn not only about how things are done but what kinds of opportunities are here for us and for our children. We look at new ways of doing things. And we start to change how we think about things. We no longer think about things the way we thought about them at home, but we learn a completely different way of thinking about things. And we not only learn a new way of thinking about things, but we learn new kinds of things to think about.

In this way immigration is like doing science. In everyday life we use science but we don't think about every day life in scientific terms. Too many immigrants learn some things about their new land, but never learn how think in terms of being part of their new land.

Both science and immigration bring new ways of looking at the world. Both bring a new set of values with which to make sense of the world.

In science we are always guided by the evidence. If the evidence does not fit our hypothesis, we must abandon our old hypothesis and develop a new one which is consistent with the existing evidence. And on further investigation we may have to go through this process again.

The most important message we can learn from science is that we can always learn new things. Old ideas can and will be overthrown.

And the same can be the case for immigration. As we continue to live in our new countries, we must learn to abandon old beliefs and adopt new ones.

This is not to say that our old beliefs have no value. They do. But by holding on to them in a different land, they may prevent us from becoming a part of our new culture.

So the big issue is trying to understand the processes that can lead to better understanding, and acceptance, of differences. But, as we look at what is happening in the world, we see that people do not always behave rationally or, in a way we would consider morally. All too often people put their short-term concerns ahead of the bigger picture and reject looking at other people in a rational moral manner.

In addition to personal reactions to these issues there is also the concern of resources. A host country may not have the physical or financial resources to take care of a great number of refugees or immigrants. This concern can also lead to anti immigrant or anti refugee views. One possible solution to the resource issue to see the issue in international terms, especially since things like wars and famines are a main cause of these migrations. An international body such as The United Nations could be put in charge of settling these migrants.

Our problem then becomes trying to understand the various reactions people have against accepting immigrants and refugees, even when they know it is the right thing to do. This is not the place to speculate on people's motives, but we can look at some historical and political trends to see why people reject immigrants and refugees.

In various places we hear terms like racial or social purity. We also hear about fears of differences. Terms like purity are clearly racist and racism is nothing new in human affairs, whether it is against people of different religious or ethnic backgrounds or of different skin color.

Another issue is globalization or other various political and economic alliances. In these situations, people tend to lose sight of their identities. Back when the European Union was being formed I argued that if an organization gets too large, people will not be able to identify with it and their identifications will get smaller. Thus instead of identifying, say, as a French person, one will then identify as, say, a Provencal person. So we go from nation to region. And smaller identities lead to less awareness of the rest of the world and to an inward rather than outward look. And this, in turn, can lead to an exclusionary view.

The main problem with exclusionary views is that they conflict with cultural and social realities. For example, in the United States there are people of color, both black, largely descendants of slaves, but also new immigrants, and brown, largely from Latin America. There also people from all over Europe, who came at different times. There are descendants of Irish immigrants, Italian immigrants, German immigrants, Chinese immigrants, and so on. In many cities we see these groups initially living in a ghetto but later generations assimilate and move throughout the country.

The point here is that one cannot maintain exclusionary views since those views come up against realities of immigrants' lives. Therefore, one must learn to accept immigration and see that eventually the children of immigrants will, at least to some extent, assimilate into the larger culture.

So, to return to our basic concepts, we have peoples of different cultures trying to live alongside each other. To be moral we try to apply the moral concepts discussed above to try to reach accommodations with these differences. These accommodations must be made on both sides.

Now to apply these concepts to refugees. Many of the same comments will apply, but because refugees leave their homelands for different reasons that immigrants, those differences have to be addressed.

The two main reasons why people are forced to leave their homelands these days are war and natural disasters such as earthquakes and floods. Some of these disasters can be attributed to climate change, but here we are only looking at the reasons people are forced to move.

Right now the biggest concern over refugees is in Europe, where people from Syria are running from war. Because Syrians are Muslim, many people in Europe are opposed to allowing these refugees entry into their Christian countries. Hungary has closed its borders; other countries are hesitant about letting more refugees in. Germany has allowed the most but there is a backlash there, and immigration of all kinds is a big issue in Britain.

What this reaction shows is a closed attitude which can be called racism or xenophobia or tribalism or nativism, or perhaps all four. We also see this in countries which have a tradition of accepting immigrants. Witness the anti immigrant views in the United States. There are a number of reasons for these attitudes. One is the fear that peoples with very different beliefs and practices will cause disruptions to the existing social order. This is certainly the case in homogenous societies. But the outrage, if one can use that term, seems a bit much. Certainly racism is at play, as is fear of what is different.

But refugees have little choice in where they end up. They must leave their homelands. That is why they are refugees.

So what can be done? We have seen, from a moral point of view, immigrants and refugees should be accepted. But we have also seen that various attitudes prevent this acceptance.

One possible solution is to make the issue of dealing with refugees an international approach, whereby a group of nations, perhaps under the umbrella of the United Nations, takes up the responsibility for resettling the refugees, or perhaps for paying for the settlements in the countries they arrive in. This may alleviate some of the problems, but it will not do away with people's negative attitudes. Of course, over time, when people see that the refugees do not cause problems, these attitudes may change.

Of course, another way to solve the problem is to stop the warring that leads to these migrations. That, too, can be a United Nations undertaking. But that may be a bit of wishful thinking if the political will of the countries involved is lacking such an undertaking.

So where are we? The big issue is the discrepancy between what is moral and people's personal beliefs. Or the discrepancy is between thinking in a truly rational selfless manner and thinking in a not so rational personal manner.

The only way that we can overcome narrow thinking is by education. But that, too, may be wishful thinking. It is great to have cultural beliefs that profess morality, but because of our individualistic societies, it is all too easy to ignore those beliefs when they are seen to conflict with personal concerns. And this brings us back to the whole idea of the relation between the culture and the individual.

My main argument has been that our source of values comes from how our cultures develop. Different cultures develop different values. The issue of multiculturism is how members of one culture mix with members of another culture. We have seen that in many cases this works out fine, but in other cases it does not work out well.

Much of the problem of why it does not work out appears to be cases of inward-looking cultures or of cultural situations which encourage strong individualism, where this individualism sees other views, other peoples, as different. In extreme cases this leads to xenophobia and/or racism. But an inward-looking culture can also lead to these ends as well.

While there may not be any easy answers to solving problems of xenophobia and racism, at least we can come to an understanding, from a moral standpoint, of how to accept the principles of multiculturism. This would involve the notion of looking at issues from the perspective of the other person, as we have discussed above. One person, or culture, sees another as "different." The other person or culture sees the first person or culture as different. If a person from the first culture tries to see his own culture as "different," from the perspective of the other culture, perhaps some understanding can be reached.

We now have to look at how nations deal with other nations. Here I want to refer to Thomas Aquinas who saw nations as individuals and believed that there was a set of moral norms that would bear on the relationships between them. Aquinas saw each nation as a collective entity with a moral and legal personality of its own.

So, when different nations deal with each other, the same kinds of moral considerations should come into play, as when individuals deal with each other. Each nation must recognize the differences in other nations and respect those differences, just like each person must respect other persons.

Aquinas sees peace as the moral norm and war as a breach of the peace—as a breach in morality. We met Aquinas above in the discussion of natural law theory. While we, of course, cannot deny that there have been wars and that there are wars going on, war is seen in a negative light. We can argue that war is a result of a breakdown of moral thought, in that the warring countries do not respect each other as moral equals.

There are many different reasons for going to war, as mentioned in chapter two. All of the aggressive actions—the starters of the war—can be seen as breaking a moral code by not recognizing the other country as a moral equal.

Another issue here is how nations deal with others when it comes to how each nation perceives the other. For example, most countries in the west claim to value human rights and also claim to abhor the mistreatment of people in other countries.

To use an analogy, let us say we live in a multicultural society that values differences. We come across an isolated homogenous society which has a very rigid view of the world. If they do not want to have any dealings with us, fine. But if they do, that is, if they want to enter into our multicultural world, they must make adaptations to their behavior. If not, we can decide to leave them alone.

However, in the world today we must deal with such societies, largely because they have resources we want or need. So we hold our noses or close our eyes and deal with them.

And, again, we see that politics, or economics, or whatever leads to aggression, breaks the rules of reason and morality, where such cultural norms override moral considerations.

CONCLUSIONS

The metaphysics of multiculturism looked at the pros and cons of accepting immigrants and/or refugees into our culture.

The epistemology showed that immigration works but there are problems with refugees, especially regarding resources.

Values show that, from a moral standpoint, we should be prepared to accept immigrants and refugees as our moral equals, especially when put the reverse test into practice. How would we want to be treated if we were the immigrant or refugee?

And using logic we tried to show how accepting immigrants and refugees could or should work. But we also found that because of some cultural beliefs, some cultures will never accept other cultures as equals. Thus, in some cases, deeply held cultural beliefs cannot be challenged by data or logic.

But we can be optimistic. We have seen in the past that consensus on a broad range of issues can be reached. So by continuing the conversations there is hope that these separating beliefs can be overcome.

And to show how this can be achieved, here some examples. For example, in the Canadian parliament there are members from many different backgrounds and ethnicities. There is a First Nations member, a turban wearing practicing Sikh, other turbaned members reflecting different ethnicities and religions, as well as people of color.

In the American congress there are people of color, Muslim and Jewish members, as well as a first-generation immigrant.

And in the relationships between countries, France and Germany, in their various guises though the centuries have been enemies since the Middles Ages, but have been great allies since the end of the Second World War.

Thus relations between people and nations can change.

NOTES

1. Canadian Multiculturalism Act–R.S.C., 1985, c. 24 (4th Supp.) (Section 3), Justice Laws Website. Government of Canada, 1985, https://www.laws-lois.justice.gc.ca/eng/acts//c-18.7/page-1.htm#h-73130. Site checked July 31.2020.

2. Carla Valle Painter, "Sense of Belonging: Literature Review," Statistics Canada, Government of Canada, June 2013. https://www.canada.ca/en/immigration-refugees-citizenship/corporate/reports-statistics. Site checked July 31.2020.

3. "Multiculturalism Policies in Contemporary Democracies United States," Multiculturalism Policy Index, Queens University. https://www.queensu.ca.mcp/immigrant-minorities/evidence/united-states. Site checked July 31.2020.

4. Hein de Haas, Stephen Castles and Mark J. Miller, *The Age of Migration* companion 4th edition website, Chapter 12.3. Macmillan Publishers Ltd. www.age-of-migration.com/uk/casestudies. Site checked July 31.2020.

5. "Multiculturalism Policies in Contemporary Democracies Netherlands," Multiculturalism Policy Index, Queens University, https://www.queensu.ca/mcp/immigrant-minorities/evidence/netherlands. Site checked July 31.2020.

6. "Dutch Politician Pim Fortuyn Assassinated," The Guardian website. Guardian News & Media Ltd., May 06, 2002, https://www.theguardian.com/world/2002/may/06/3. Site checked July 31.2020.

7. "The Changing Face of the Country," Spiegel International website. Spiegel International. April 19, 2018, www.spiegel.de/international/germany/germany-ans-immigration-the-changing-face-of-the-country. Site checked July 31.2020.

Chapter Three

Sex and Gender

This is a set of related issues, ranging from whether or not men and women are equal, and if so in what ways, to the relation between sex, which is biological, and gender, which is biological and social, to issues around same sex and transgender relationships, and whether same sex relationships are natural or not.

METAPHYSICS

Western civilization has long maintained a strong distinction between men and women. From Ancient Greece through the twentieth century Western societies have been patriarchal, with women being relegated to secondary roles regarding motherhood. Many women were not permitted to leave their homes unaccompanied. Throughout history and in many societies women have had to keep their heads covered. And as we get to the modern era women are still seen as second-class citizens. When entering the workforce they are paid less than men for the same jobs, usually on the grounds that they will get pregnant and leave, so there is no point in investing in them.

Much of this view of women is based on the fact that women can get pregnant and have to look after their children, especially in the formative years when they are nursing. It is this idea that led to the notion that biology is destiny, that women were destined to be mothers, and as a result, second class citizens.

One of the issues that have been part of western civilization almost from the beginning has been for women to deny their second-class status and fight for equality.

The other set of issues we will look at here revolves around same sex issues. We will look at the nature of same sex behavior and the rights that go along with our understanding of such behavior.

EPISTEMOLOGY

Knowledge about these issues will come from a number of sources: history, psychology, anthropology, sociology, and biology.

We will see that even though women have been put in this second-class position, they have constantly challenged this view. We will look at anthropology to see how some of these social roles have changed. We will look at sociology to see how social orders are organized and how these structures are being challenged. And we will look at biology to see if the differences that are claimed are in fact embedded in our biology or are they found in our social structures.

Biology will also play an important role in looking at issues revolving around same sex behavior.

VALUES

Values play two different roles here. On the one hand we will look at the values behind supporting the second-class role of women, and on the other hand we will look at the values behind challenging this status.

Much of the defense of the second-class status of women comes from two sources—tradition and religion. And often one is used to support the other.

We can say that the intent of the defenders of the position is to simply maintain their status, or to maintain the social status quo. They fear the possible consequences of changes in the status of women and in the relationships between men and women that would occur as a result of these changes.

And we can say that the intent of women looking for change is simply to acknowledge their humanity and that there is no good reason for maintaining the subjugation of women. They see the possible consequences of these changes in a positive light.

These comments also apply to same sex behavior issues. The views against the acceptance of such behaviors also come from both a fear of change, and a conservative view of religion which, if we go back to the story of Noah, we see nature as binary, male and female. Indeed, the Noachid commandments speak against same sex behavior. The book of Leviticus states "Thou shalt not lie with mankind, as with womankind; it is an abomination." And in the next chapter it states, "Though shalt not let thy cattle gender with a diverse kind; thou shalt not sow thy field with two kinds of seed; neither shall there come upon a garment with two kinds of stuff mingled together." It is easy to quote one passage and ignore the others, but wearing a garment made of two kinds of cloth, or planting more than one crop in a field, is seen in a similar light to lying with mankind as with womankind.

LOGIC

Here we will evaluate the various arguments in the light of the knowledge and values presented.

DISCUSSION

Let us start with history. I would like to begin with the story of Lilith. There are a number of versions of the story, some seeing Lilith in a positive light, others in a negative light. But all stories agree that Lilith wanted to be acknowledged as Adam's equal. When Adam refused this, Lilith left, and this is where the stories diverge. The point to be made here is that if Lilith's demand was legitimate, then the story shows that at one time men and women were equals, but, over time, that changed, and women ended up in a subservient position to men, as we see in the creation of Eve, who was created out of Adam, and so was created to be subservient.

The question then becomes, what led to this change in the status of women? Anthropologists primarily see the culprit in the development of agriculture. But in order to fully appreciate the changes in social organization, we must go back to Freud and his influence on anthropology.

Freud saw civilization developing out of what he calls the primal horde, where sons fight for leadership and in so doing kill their fathers. This leads to a notion of guilt and the development of the two great taboos: murder and incest, which is the theme of *Totem and Taboo*.

Robin Fox looks at Freud's work and argues that Freud and the anthropologists who have been influenced by him have been asking the wrong question. By asking the question in terms of why there is such a horror about incest, Fox sees them as begging the question in that the assumption is that incest is widespread. But he argues this is not the case. So Fox rephrases the question in terms of why humans do not commit much incest. Since there are examples of incest in nature and in humans, the question becomes one of where and when is it appropriate. Fox also develops the argument to show that the incest taboo is linked to exogamy—marrying outside of one's group. There is a great deal of evidence that people learn early on not to mate with people from their own groups. Fox and others like Jack Goody, and M. R. Chance, argue that there is a biological basis for this, coming out of Darwin's notion of natural selection, for diversity is biologically important.[1]

It is this point that leads to the development of kinship relationships. Humans had to learn to control hostile impulses, especially those directed at other people and not prey. The unconscious controls that develop also go into developing our social and personality structures. The results of these psychological and behavioral restraints take the form of kinship relations and sexual-social roles. Kinship systems are not just about families, they are about "relationships set up between people who exchange spouses according to a set of rules,"[2] There can be many different forms of kinship relations but there will always be rules governing them.

And, Fox continues, in the context of hunting, come sex roles. Men and women take on specific roles. Fox here follows Freud. While he does not use the term "anatomy is destiny" he uses the concept. "The male-female division of labor has to do with vegetable foods, which the women gather, and animal protein obtained by men. . ."[3]

Fox goes on to argue that such behavior also is exhibited in primates, but in humans, because of our larger brains and our self-awareness, our understanding of our sexuality moved from the purely biological to the emotional. It is this evolutionary development which allows for the Freudian notion of guilt to control our social organization.

And now we look at Marvin Harris again, who re-interprets Freud and disagrees with Fox. Harris agrees that cultures take diverse forms but argues that these forms are not the result of chance.

> I think there is an intelligible process that governs the maintenance of common cultural forms, initiates changes, and determines their transformation along parallel or divergent paths. The heart of the process is the tendency to intensify production.[4]

Harris sees increased food production as a response to various threats to culture. Such threats include changes to climates, people migrations and competition for resources. Harris argues that while intensification is initially successful, it usually ends up being counterproductive since it leads to the depletion of the environment.

The issue has to do with increasing population and the need to feed more people. If food sources could not increase, populations had to decrease. Fertility could be controlled with diet. Harris shows that low fertility is linked with diets that are high in protein and low in carbohydrates. High protein allows a mother to nurse longer, thereby delaying her fertile period.[5]

Most early cultures were hunter-gatherers, or, as Harris likes to call them gatherer-hunters, since more of the food came from gathering than from hunting. The main reason for the shift from gathering and hunting to agriculture had to do with the depletion of animal protein sources.

Agricultural cultures take many forms. The form will always be determined by the relationship between the population and the food supply. Thus biological survival and reproduction are the determining factors in the structure of a culture. Biological survival also, of course, involves adaptation to one's environment.

Scarcity of food or competition for food can lead to war. Wars between gatherer-hunters are nowhere near as fierce as wars between agricultural communities for two reasons: one is that when communities are permanent, there is a defense of the land involved, and two, agricultural communities tend to be larger than gatherer-hunter communities so more people are involved in the fighting. But Harris asks why people fight. Following Ashley Montague, he argues that there are no instincts or dispositions in people to kill others.

So why do we kill? Harris looks to the question of fertility. If populations could be controlled there would be no need to compete for food. Thus, fertility is the key. In a group of ten women and one man there could be ten births. In a group of ten men and ten women there would be ten births. In a group of ten men and one woman there would be one birth. Thus, as Harris argues, "the number of women determines the rate of fertility."[6] In times of war fighters are needed, which leads to a strong patriarchal social structure. Thus Harris argues,

> That without reproductive pressure neither warfare nor female infanticide would have become widespread and that the conjunction of the two represents a savage but uniquely effective solution to the Malthusian dilemma.[7]

But, as Harris continues, other factors come into play regarding the roles of men and women. For the most part, in gatherer-hunter societies women are more highly valued.

> After all, women can do that most of the things men can do, and they alone can bear and nurse infants. Men on average may be heavier, stronger, and faster runners than women, but in favorable habitats there are few production processes in which these physiological features make men more decisively effective than women. . . . Women hunters could easily substitute for men without reducing the supply of high-quality protein. And several recent studies have shown that among horticulturists women provide more calories and proteins in the form of

food plants and small animals even if they don't hunt big game... The explanation for the near universal exclusion of women from big game hunting appears to lie in the practice of warfare, the male-supremacist sex roles which arise in conjunction with warfare, and the practice of female infanticide—all of which ultimately derive from the attempt to solve the problem of reproductive pressure.[8]

So the social roles of men and women are not due to their sex, i.e., their anatomy, but to social evolution regarding population increase and food supply. So, unlike Freud, Harris sees social and sexual roles dependent on the nature of culture and its relationship to the physical environment. To develop this point further let us look at a study by anthropologist Patricia Draper who was quoted in chapter one, regarding the different divisions of labor in a gatherer-hunter society and an agricultural society.

When we look at the work of Harris and Draper we see that anatomy is not destiny and that our sexual roles—our genders—are products of cultural and environmental factors.

We must briefly mention Freud here since his work will come up again later. Freud is important because of his influence on anthropology, especially in his work, *Totem and Taboo* and *Civilization and its Discontents*, where he looked at the origins of culture and the role of guilt in keeping our behaviors in line.

While Harris acknowledges Freud's influence, he also argues that Freud got the causal arrows wrong. Freud began with the individual and argued that, due to individual psychology, culture was created. Whereas, Harris, and anthropologists in general, argue that it is culture that creates individualistic psychology. To be specific, Freud saw the problems arising from the Oedipus complex—where the son wants to kill his father and marry his mother—led to the kind of aggression that led to warfare, while Harris sees the state of war, or readiness for war as the cause of the complex.

Now that we have looked at the origins of gender roles, we begin looking at women's fight for equality in the light of western civilization.

But a number of points need to be made here. Two of them have to do with biological factors: Are male and female brains different? And does testosterone make male behavior different from female behavior? While we see that the large social roles are social and not sexual in nature, people still claim there are significant differences between men and women, and these differences still justify different treatments. These two points, depending on how they are used, can lead to different views on the relationship between men and women and on their respective roles.

In her excellent book T*estosterone Rex*: *Myths of Sex, Science, and Society*, Cordelia Fine argues, using various studies that the arguments about men being able to do certain things or that they act in certain ways is based in biology, namely testosterone, are largely myths and that the behaviors in question are in fact socially constructed. And Gina Rippon has shown in her recent work that there is virtually no difference between the brains of men and women.

Fine begins her argument by recapping the various reasons given for treating men and women differently, from how evolutionary views about sexual selection are unconsciously being used today to justify treating men and women differently. She goes on to argue,

> When we think of men and women in this complementary way, it's intuitive to look for a single, powerful case that creates this divide between the sexes. And if you're thinking right now of a hormone beginning with the letter T, you're not alone. Testosterone has long featured prominently in explanations of differences between the sexes, and continues to do so.[9]

She then asks,

> So what does it mean for hopes of equality if testosterone fuels the appetite for adventure? Of *course* we should value the special qualities that arise from women's low risk, low stakes approach to life. As world economies struggle to recover from the reckless risk taking that brought about the global financial crisis, commentators ask if there is "too much testosterone" on Wall Street, calling for more senior women in finance. To a woman, after all, with the merest dribble of testosterone coursing through her bloodstream, subprime mortgages and complex credit derivatives will not have the same irresistible appeal. But here's the other side of that coin. If, thanks to the hand of evolution and implemented by testosterone, one sex is biologically more predisposed to want to take risks and get ahead, then it simply stands to reason that this is the sex that will be more eager to, say, take on the gamble of entrepreneurship. . . or to aspire to a powerful status. . .[10]

But, Fine goes on to argue,

> While the genetic and hormonal components of sex certainly influence brain development and function—we are not asexual blank slates—sex is just one of many interacting factors. We are an adapted species of course, but also unusually adaptable. Beyond genitals, sex is surprisingly dynamic, and not just open to influence from gender constructions, but reliant on them. Nor does sex inscribe us with male brains and female brains, or with male or female characteristics—not even when it comes to risk taking and competitiveness, the traits so often called upon to explain why men are more likely to rise to the top.[11]

And Fine concludes that testosterone is not the king or kingmaker of masculinity that is it often assumed to be.[12]

She begins her discussion by citing Angus Bateman's famous experiment with fruit flies, based on his interpretation of Darwin's notion of sexual selection, where he concluded that, based on the number of offspring, there was greater male variation in the offspring, which leads to the view that male promiscuity benefits the species.[13]

Until very recently these conclusions, along with the basic assumptions of male-female differences, went unchallenged. But in 2007 Brian Snyder and Patricia Galloway tried to redo the experiment. They found that some of Bateman's assumptions colored his data towards a male bias and found that Bateman only reported data that supported his assumptions.[14]

Once these assumptions were challenged observers started to find different patterns. Sarah Blaffer Hrdy was surprised to find female langurs behaving promiscuously. At first she admits she had no context for this behavior that seemed strange but in time came to realize that such behaviors were normal for langurs.[15]

An important point that needs developing is the notion that sex is not just biological but also social. As Jonathon Marks points out "To confuse human (cultural) sexuality and (natural) reproduction is classically pseudo-scientific. Of course, sexuality is for reproduction—if you're a lemur. If you're a human, sexuality is far more than for reproduction; that is what evolution has done for human nature. He goes on to say that "if you imagine sex to be biological rather than bio-cultural, you're probably not going to have much of it."[16]

And Fine then quotes Carol Travis from her book *The Mismeasure of Woman*,

> Our sexuality is body, culture, age learning, habit, fantasies, worries, passions, and the relationships in which all these elements combine. That's why sexuality can change with age, partner, experience, emotions, and sense of perspective.[17]

And to anticipate Rippon's work, after reviewing many other studies Fine argues:

> So sex does indeed matter, but in a complicated and unpredictable way. Although there *are* sex effects that create differences in the brain, sex *isn't* the basic, determining factor in brain development that is for the reproductive system. Unlike the genitals, "human brains cannot be categorized into two distinct classes: male brain/ female brain." quoting Daphna Joel.[18]

To return to the main theme of Fine's book, quoting from a study of a cichlid fish known as *haplochromis burtoni*, in which Richard Francis and colleagues took a male dominant fish with large testicles and castrated it and then put it in a tank with more submissive males, and it still continued to dominate, concluding that even in such fish, testosterone is not an omnipotent player. "If it were, then castrating a territorial fish would be a guaranteed method of bringing about his social downfall. But it isn't."[19]

So if testosterone is not just about maleness or male aggressiveness or male dominance, what is it for?

Fine argues that it is complicated and does play a role in courtship and mating. Testosterone can regulate various bodily functions which can affect the brain with regard to mating behaviors. And testosterone also binds to nerve cells and can affect how nerve cells function.[20]

But her main conclusion, based on a number of carefully conducted studies, is that most of what we call male behavior is socially conditioned and not determined by testosterone.

Which brings us to the brain. Gina Rippon reviews all the brain studies and shows how they are based on assumptions of differences between men and women and that whatever is found is used to support these assumptions.[21] She discusses a study using imaging which showed that men and women had different connections in their brains: Men had stronger connections within hemispheres for men and stronger connections between hemispheres for women. But the study did not show whether men and women actually exhibited these differences. "Measurements of brain connectivity were being filtered through preconceived, stereotypical beliefs."[22]

> More importantly is the point that we are studying adult brains and not understanding the process of development.
>
> Scientists used to think that beyond the changes that occur during the highly plastic early years of the brain, and barring deviations caused by damage, disease or deprivation, you generally end up with the brain you were born with, only bigger and better connected.
>
> We now know this isn't the case. Our brains are very much a product of the lives we have lived, the experiences we have had, and our education, occupations, sports and hobbies. The way we perform tasks reflects not just the running of predetermined internal software, but also external inputs.[23]

And, finally,

> Revisiting the evidence suggests that women and men are more similar than they are different.[24]

But, of course, there are differences between the sexes—if only the fact that women get pregnant and men do the impregnating. But, once we can control fertility, especially through effective means of birth control, these differences become less important.

Now that we have seen that women and men are more equal than traditional views have held, let us look at some of the history of women and their attempts to demonstrate this equality. This discussion is based on *A Brief History of Feminism* by Patu and Antje Schrupp.

In Ancient Greece the playwright Menander in 342 or 343 wrote that "A man who teaches a woman how to read or write is ill-advised, for he is providing extra venom to an asp." Yet we have some fragmentary traces of poetry written by women as early as the seventh and sixth centuries BCE, mainly from the island of Lesbos, and Plato mentions a woman philosopher named Diotima as an alleged teacher of Socrates, though no other source exists for her.

In the Hebrew tradition, women had a secondary role, and, to this day, in Orthodox congregations, women and men cannot sit together. However there are traditions of strong women such as the prophet Miriam and the political leader Esther. In Christianity, Paul said women should be silent, which he would not have needed to say if women had not been silent. In early Christianity there was, of course, Mary Magdalene, who should have been considered a true disciple if she had been male—witness the Gospel of Mary—and other apostates such as Junia and Thekia. In the fourth century CE the mathematician Hypatia was murdered by fanatical Christian monks.

During the Middle Ages, there were a number of prominent women. One of the most famous was Abbess Hildegard von Bingen (1098–1170). And in 1280 Wilhelmina of Milan had a vision which challenged the male hierarchy of the church, but she was burned as a heretic in 1300. And from that period women stared to make their voices known. Women started to live together to support each other and became known as "Beguines"—the most famous was Frenchwoman Marguerite Porete, (ca 1260–1310) who wrote the first major spiritual work in the vernacular language, entitled *The Mirror of Simple Souls*, which argues that God can be found not through the church or through reason but through an individual's ability to love.

In the early modern era as science started to displace religion, men still found ways to subjugate women by using science, claiming that science demonstrated women to be inferior beings. In 1405 French writer Christine de Pizan published *The Book of the City Ladies* which attacks misogynist thinking that claims women have fewer aptitudes.

> They who defame women are small spirits. They have encountered so many women ranking far above them in terms of wisdom and gentility that their reaction is to be sulky and indignant. And because of this grudge, they speak ill of women.[25]

The so-called women question was debated through the next few centuries and the argument became more polarized, with women demanding more education and the abolition of forced marriages. An important thinker in this period was French philosopher Marie de Gournay (1565–1645).

> Biological differences in sex do not account for the spirit of a human being, rather, they serve only for procreation. After all, this female cat on my windowsill cannot be distinguished from a tomcat.[26]

> A logical consequence is the right of women to be human, for in principle then human spirit is neither masculine nor feminine.(*The Equality of Women*, 1622).

In the eighteenth century, especially after the French Revolution, men maintained their superior status, but by the nineteenth century women started to fight back. The first strong voice for the equality of women was Mary Wollstonecraft, who wrote A *Vindication of the Rights of Women* in 1792, in part as a reaction to Edmund Burke's *Reflections on the French Revolution* in which he praised old views of authority and tradition.

> I may excite laughter, by dropping an hint, which I mean to pursue some future time, for I really think women ought to have representatives, instead of being arbitrarily governed without having any direct share allowed them in the deliberations of government.[27]

And in 1818 Mary Wollstonecraft's daughter Mary Shelley wrote *Frankenstein*, which can be seen as criticizing the male hubris of science. Today it is read as a feminist book with the monster as the woman demanding equality, thus being shunned by society.

In France in 1791 human rights activist Marie Gouze (1748–1793) known by her pen name Olympe de Gouges, wrote the *Declaration of the Rights of Woman and the Female Citizen*.

Her best known "bon mot" is "A woman who has the right to ascend to the scaffold must also have the right to ascend a political platform."[28]

By the beginning of the nineteenth century the notion of "equality of all men" had actually widened the chasm not only between men and women but also between the rich and poor. As we see today, laws were made by the privileged for themselves, which left everyone else to their own devices. A reaction to this was the development of various socialist movements which dreamed of greater equality between men and women and between rich and poor. In the early nineteenth century a movement known as Saint Simonism, after sociologist Henri de Saint-Simon, which argued that gender specific characteristics were not given by nature but were attributable to unequal socialization

One of the most important women of this movement was Claire Demar (1799–1833).

Precisely because woman is equal to man but not identical to him, she should participate in the effort for social reform, and in so doing she will embody the necessary elements that men lacks, such that the endeavor can be complete.[29]

The Saint-Simonists went on to develop models for gender-conscious organizational structures and founded various women's groups. In this context an important theorist was Flora Tristan (1803–1844) who fled her violent husband since she had no legal option for a divorce. On a trip to Peru she rebelled against slavery and in 1840 she travelled to London and researched and wrote about the living conditions of workers under capitalism. In 1843, five years before Marx wrote the Communist Manifesto, Tristan's The Workers' Union was published in which she championed the idea of a union of male and female workers. She also drew a link between the oppression of women and the oppression of the proletariat.

One can only wonder that if it were not for the general prejudice against women we would we talking about Saint-Simonism or Tristanism today instead of Marxism.

The next major development in feminism comes from the United States in 1848 when "The First Convention ever called to discuss the Civil and Political Rights of Women" occurred in Seneca Falls N.Y. on July 19 and 20. The main initiators of the conference were Lucrezia Mott (1793–1880) and Elizabeth Cady Stanton (1815–1902). Approximately three hundred people attended, including black civil rights activist Frederick Douglass.

The conference issued a "declaration of Rights and Sentiments" echoing the American declaration of Independence.

> Thomas Jefferson wrote in his Declaration of Independence that all men are created equal. And we are hereby declaring that all men and women are also created equal by Nature and are therefore endowed with the same rights.[30]

And this was followed by Elizabeth Cady Stanton claiming that,

> We insist that women have immediate admission to all the rights and privileges which belong to them as citizens of these United States. In entering upon the great work before us, we anticipate no small amount of misconception, misrepresentation, and ridicule; but we shall use every instrumentality within our power to affect our object.[31]

Europe also saw similar movements with several national assemblies taking place.

This feminist action led to a tremendous backlash, which, in turn provoked even more feminist writing. Two important writers of the time were Juliette Adam (1838–1936) who wrote *Anti Proudhonist Ideas about Love, Women and Marriage* in 1858, and Hedwig Dohm (1831–1919) who wrote *The Antifeminists* in 1902.

At the US women's conference in 1851, itinerant preacher and former slave Sojourner Truth (1798–1883) gave a speech in which she debunked the idea of "positive discrimination" favoring women as a "weaker" sex in need of protection and also denounced the racism inherent in bourgeois clichés about gender.

The next issue that women started to talk about was labor and wages, which was the result of women entering the labor market. Men's unions were hostile to allowing women into their ranks.

So women organized to push for their own benefits and challenged the various "women's protection laws" which prevented women from working various jobs due to their supposedly inferior constitutions. In England in 1859 women organized the Society for Promoting the Employment of Women. And in Germany journalist Louise Otto-Peters launched a women's newspaper in 1849 and also founded workers' and servant' unions. Her book, *Right to Earn a Living*, was published in 1866.

Back in England Harriet Taylor Mill and her daughter Helen Taylor, together with philosopher John Stuart Mill, actively pursued the equality of women. The most famous work of this group, which was published under John Stuart Mill's name, was *The Subjection of Women*.

"The legal subordination of one sex to the other is wrong in itself, and now one of the chief hindrances to human improvement."[32]

The next issue women took on was marriage. In the nineteenth century, and, of course, much earlier as well, married women had no standing of their own. When married they virtually became property of their husbands, and all their property became the property of the husband as well. But this led to differences within the feminist movement where some women, such as Minna Cauer, Lida Gustava Heyman, Anita Augspurg and Helene Stocker, and George Sand, wanted to challenge the whole family and moral structure, while others, such as Helene Lange and Gertrud Baumer, while opposed to forced marriage laws and the unjust treatment of men, argued for the maintenance of the role of women in her social and maternal roles.

Then came the issue of the right to vote. By the nineteenth century many men still could not vote as voting was tied to owning property, so the movement to expand voting rights included working men as well as women. In the United States splits came when there were attempts to allow black men to vote. Some people would rather give the vote to white women before they would give it to black men.

In England the suffragette movement forced the issue into the mainstream. However, New Zealand was the first country to give women the vote in 1893, followed by Australia in 1902, Finland in 1906, Norway in 1913, 1920 in the United States, 1928 in Britain and Ireland, 1945 in France and Italy, and 1971 in Switzerland.

In the post World War Two years, all kinds of things happened, which directly affected women. The first book to really deal with the equality of women was Simone de Beauvoir's *The Second Sex*, published in 1949, which argued that women were equals to men, and showed how women's roles were defined by men not only in legislation but in literature, morality and everyday customs. De Beauvoir's book did not become really influential for two decades after the new women's movement developed, largely in the United States and Canada.

These developments in women's rights came with the new prosperity that was developing. People were moving to the suburbs. One of the consequences of this move was that women became isolated. In the city, women who were stay at home housewives could go shopping on their own, socialize with other women and lead busy lives. But in the suburbs, where houses were farther apart, and where there was no public transportation, stay at home women were isolated. This led to various behaviors including drinking. In 1963 Betty Friedan published *The Feminine Mystique*, which chronicled this problem with no name, as it came to be known. Women who were isolated, and who were part of an individualistic society blamed themselves for their behaviors. Many women got part time jobs to help add to the family income and support their new lifestyles, and found they were not being paid the same as men were paid for the same work. But when it was demonstrated that their behaviors were part of a larger social phenomenon, that women generally were not being paid equally, their views changed, and this led to a decade of feminist development which was later called the "second wave" after the wave that guaranteed women's voting rights.

The late 1960s and early 1970s saw many books about the changing roles of women. In France we saw books by Luce Irigaray and Julia Kristeva.[33,34] In the United States we saw a Marxist analysis of feminism from Shulamith Firestone,[35] and political analysis from Kate Millett and from Germaine Greer.[36,37] And bell hooks and Patricia Hill offer an African American perspective.

Discussion of all aspects of women's lives took place, from politics, to abortion, to spousal abuse. Various pieces of legislation were passed in response to some of these issues. But women still had a long way to go to attain equality.

At this time there was also a movement to acknowledge gay and lesbian rights starting with the Stonewall Riots in New York in 1969. The women's movement quickly picked up on this and took on lesbian politics as part of their issues.

Coming out of Friedan's work was the optimistic psychology of Abraham Maslow. It was thought that if women were to become the persons they could be—if they could self-actualize—they could attain equality. But women soon found out that self-actualizing was not enough. They had to deal with social and political realities which were still being controlled by men.

In order to properly analyze this situation a depth psychology was needed. So women had to go back to Freud even though they didn't like much of what he said about women. Freud had maintained what has been called "the one sex model" in that women were seen as mirror images of men, rather than as something in themselves. I have always believed that Freud knew he was wrong about women but did not know how to get out of his model, which is why he encouraged women to become psychoanalysts.

And it is a woman who picks up on Freud's themes to help women understand the social situation they were in.

The reason humanistic psychology could not understand the social structures people found themselves in was because this approach deals with individual development and does not address how people function in the social world, let alone acknowledge the social dimensions of individual personalities. In a sense Maslownian humanistic psychology sees people as individual units with no place in the social world, and as a result there is no discussion of how the social world affects the development of individual personalities.

The main point here is that truly self-actualized persons are psychologically self-sufficient and self-contained and as a result do not need other people. Think of Ayn Rand's selfishness—he only thing that matters is me. Feminist writer Jean Grimshaw asks whether this means that self-actualized persons no longer need other people or if they can enter into relationships with other self-actualized people on an equal basis. Grimshaw sees self-actualized persons in the first light but sees feminism in the second light. Since one of the things that feminism is concerned about is social relationships, Grimshaw sees the self-actualized person as incompatible with feminism and as such sees the concept in masculine terms. Thus the Maslow model of self-actualization proves to be no help to feminism.

But a psychological theory of development of persons is needed. One has to be able to account for how people develop their sense of selves and how they develop a sense of others. The only theory of psychology that attempts to do this is psychoanalysis. This task in undertaken by sociologist Nancy Chodorow in her book, *The Reproduction of Mothering: Psychoanalysis and the Sociology of Gender*.

She begins with the obvious: women mother. They not only bear children but have the primary responsibility to raise them. But women also participate in the labor force and have other social roles as well. So, Chodorow wants to know "how do women today come to mother?" The implication here is that by coming to understand the role of motherhood we will come to understand how we might "transform the sexual division of labor in which women mother."[38]

The main reason for raising questions about the role of mothering has to do with the changing nature of that role. As the role of women in society has changed, so has the role of mothering. Yet with all the changes that have taken place, women still want to be mothers. Part of the reason is that, as Chodorow's title implies, mothers teach their daughters how to mother. Chodorow's point is that,

> The contemporary reproduction of mothering occurs through social structurally induced psychological processes. It is neither a product of biology nor of intentional role training. I draw on the psychoanalytic account of female and male personality development to demonstrate that women's mothering reproduces itself cyclically. Women as mothers, produce daughters with mothering capacities and the desire to mother. These capacities and needs are built into and grow out of the mother-daughter relationship itself. By contrast, women as mothers (and men as not-mothers) produce sons whose nurturant capacities and needs have been systematically curtailed and repressed. This prepares men for their less affective later family role, and for primary participation in the impersonal extra-familial world of work and public life.[39]

The important point here is that male and female roles are socially developed. Men can learn to be more nurturant. But to do so would involve changes in family life and in our overall social structures. The rest of the book is about what is involved in understanding how these structures work and how they can be changed.

An important point coming out of Chodorow's work is the distinction between sex and gender. Sex is biological but gender is social. And as the above quote points out, gender roles are taught.

Recall the story about the car crash where the father was killed and the surgeon could not operate on the boy, saying, "it is my son."

I think it would be obvious today that the answer is the boy's mother. But back in the 1980s that was not so obvious. There were not as many women doctors, so people gave all kinds of answers, from stepdad, to biological father with the driver being the stepdad, and so on. This shows what is known as systemic thinking. We live in a patriarchal society and the nature of that society determines our gender roles. But as we have been challenging the foundations of the patriarchy, we see our social roles changing.

Chodorow spends a great amount of time using the Freudian model of child development, and in so doing has revised the Freudian notion of sexuality without diminishing its importance. Her revision shows that we are biological beings but that our belief in "anatomy is destiny" has been culturally conditioned. She shows that our gender roles develop from the way we are brought up, and that by bringing up our children differently we can change how they perceive their own sexuality and their own gender roles.

Chodorow's work has been recognized as important in that is has spurred other work. She was one influence behind Carol Gilligan's work, which in turn led to numerous investigations into how women function differently from men, such as Mary Field Belenky et al., *Women's Ways of Knowing: The Development of Self, Voice and Mind.*

Chodorow's work has also been severely criticized. One criticism comes from women of color who see her work as largely referring to the white middle class, and another comes from the gay and lesbian community arguing that her work does not take their issues into account. Both sets of criticisms are important and there has been much written on them. I want to focus on the same sex issue here.

As mentioned above, in Western society same sex behavior has been looked upon as sinful and unnatural. It is mentioned as sinful going back to the story of Noah and the commandments given to him after the flood. But most of the discussion dates from the work of Thomas Aquinas who states,

> When speaking of man's nature we may refer either to that which is proper to him or to that which he has in common with other animals. From the first point of view, all sins in so far as they are against reason are also against nature, as Damascene states. From the second, some special sins are against nature, a, for instance those that run counter to the intercourse of male and female natural to animals, and so are peculiarly qualified as unnatural vices.[40]

Thus, since same sex behavior is not found in nature, it is unnatural and therefore immoral.

But current knowledge has demonstrated Aquinas' view to be false. In *Biological Exuberance*, Bruce Bagemihl has amassed a wealth of observations showing that same sex, bisexual and trans behaviors exist all through nature, from insects, to birds to small mammals, to bulls and goats to elephants and whales. As he states:

> Wild animals often form significant pair-bonds with animals of the same sex. Homosexual pair-bonding takes many different forms, but two broad categories can be recognized: "partners who engage in sexual or courtship activities with each other, and "companions" who are bonded to each other but do not necessarily engage in sexual activity with each other.[41]

He goes on to state,

> The traditional view of the animal kingdom-what might be called the Noah's ark view—is that biology revolves around two sexes, male and female, with one of each to a pair. The range of genders and sexualities actually found in the animal world, however, is considerably richer than this. Animals with females that become males, animals with no males at all, animals that are both male and female simultaneously, animals where males resemble females, animals where females court other females, and where ,ales court other males—Noah's ark was never quite like this! Homosexuality represents but one of a wide variety of alternative sexualities and genders. Many people are familiar with transvestism or transexuality only in humans, yet similar phenomenon are also found in the animal kingdom.[42]

Thus our traditional categories of male and female do not capture the true diversity of nature. They are limiting constructions which must be radically changed or abandoned if we are to truly construct socio-sexual categories which reflect nature as well as human diversity.

The women's movement continues to critique systemic sexism in all walks of life such as family structures and child raising, the world of work, both in terms of what jobs women can do and in the boardroom, and in society in general. While women have come a long way, there is still a long way to go.

CONCLUSIONS

Metaphysics

The issue here is that between looking at women in traditional ways and seeing women as individuals in their own right outside those traditional roles women have also had to overcome various stereotypes and assumptions about their natures.

We have seen that while men and women differ with regard to their roles in reproduction, they do not differ in any other important way. On the biological side, we have seen that women's brains are not significantly different from men's brains. We have seen that testosterone does not make men different from women. On the psychological side we have seen that the main differences between men and women have more to do with how they are socialized than with biology, though the need to nurture children does play a role.

We have seen through history how women have tried to demonstrate their equality to men and, gradually, they have won various battles. Systemic sexism still exists, but it is being overcome.

Epistemology

In this chapter we have seen large amounts of knowledge amassed from biology, sociology, and psychology, which shows that women are equal to men in most areas of life. One of the main arguments against women taking their rightful roles in society and in the workplace has been the fact that women get pregnant. One issue not discussed in this chapter is women's sexuality. Women, of course, have sex drives much like men do but, for much of our history, have had to learn to control those drives because of the fear of getting pregnant. But with the development of good methods of birth control, those fears no longer exist so women can now also act on their sexuality in ways equal to men.

And when it comes to same sex issues, we see that knowledge of nature shows us that same sex behavior exists all through nature, thus it is both natural and moral. One implication of this point is that sex is not just for reproduction but clearly plays a much larger role in our lives.

Indeed, sexuality is of great importance in determining how we organize our societies, how we determine our social roles and how we perceive ourselves.

Values

Values play a number of different roles here. On the one hand a set of values determined that women were not equal to men. On the other hand a set of values led women to challenge their unequal treatment. As we have seen, largely because of how women are brought up, they have developed nurturing skills and greater empathy than men, so part of the argument in making women equal is to bring these values to the fore and to transform society in the light of these nurturing values.

We have also seen how changing knowledge of what women are, from biology, psychology and sociology, has led to many of these changes. Thus many of the values that women have espoused over the centuries, but primarily in the last half-century or so, have been knowledge based, thereby challenging the separation of fact and value, by showing how knowledge leads to changing values.

Logic

Logic is used as the basis of argument to reach a sound and valid conclusion. In this chapter we have stated an issue with regard to women's equality. We then amassed a great deal of information from various historical, biological, sociological, and psychological sources to show that from all of these viewpoints, women are indeed men's equals. So we must therefore conclude that women are indeed men's equals in all walks of life, with the obvious exception of bearing children, from parenting to the worlds of work, the boardroom, government, the arts, sports, and education.

NOTES

1. Fox Robin, *The Red Lamp of Incest* (New York: E.P. Dutton. 1980).
2. Fox, 140.
3. Fox, 116.
4. Harris, Marvin, *Cannibals and Kings, The Origins of Culture*, (New York: Random House, 1987) 4.
5. Harris, 16.
6. Harris, 39.
7. Harris, 41.
8. Harris, 42.
9. Fine, Cordelia, *Testosterone Rex: Myths of Sex, Science and Society*, (London: W.W. Norton, 2017) 18.
10. Fine, 20.
11. Fine, 23.
12. Fine 23.
13. Fine, 31–32.
14. Fine, 34–36.
15. Fine, 38.
16. Fine, 65.
17. Fine, 78.
18. Fine, 92.
19. Fine, 130–131.
20. Fine, 137.
21. Rippon, Gina, *New Scientist* 2 March p 29.
22. Rippon, 30.
23. Rippon, 30.
24. Rippon, 31.
25. Patu/Schrupp Antje, *A Brief History of Feminism*, (Cambridge, MIT Press, 2017)10.
26. Patu and Schrupp, *Feminism* 12.
27. Patu and Schrupp, 15.
28. Patu and Schrupp, 18.
29. Patu and Schrupp, 22.
30. Patu and Schrupp, 26.
31. Patu and Schrupp, 26.
32. John Stuart Mill, Harriet Taylor Mill and Helen Taylor.

33. Irigaray, Luce, *An Ethics of Sexual Difference.* Trans. Carolyn Burke and Gillian C. Gill. Ithaca: Cornell Univ. Press, 1993.

34. Toril Moi, ed *The Kristeva Reader*, (New York: The Columbia University Press, 1986).

35. Firestone Shulamith, T*he Dialectic of Sex The Case for Feminist Revolution* (NewYork: Farrar Strauss Geroux, 1970).

36. Millet, Kate, *Sexual Politics* (New York: Columbia University Press, 1970).

37. Greer, Germaine, *The Female Eunuch* (New York: Harper, 2008).

38. Chodorow, Nancy, *The Reproduction of Mothering*: *Psychoanalysis and the Sociology of Gender*, (Berkeley: University of California Press, 1978) 4.

39. Chodorow, 7.

40. St. Thomas Aquinas, *Summa Theologica*, 94.2.

41. Bagemihl, Bruce, Bi*ological Exuberance*: *Animal Homosexuality and Natural Diversity*, (New York: Saint Martin's Press, 1999), 20.

42. Bagemihl, 36.

Chapter Four

Issues of Life and Death
Abortion and Euthanasia

I put these two issues together because some people see them as two sides of the same coin, while others see them as two separate issues. I will deal with them as two separate issues, but will discuss why some people see them in the same light.

Both issues deal with aspects of life and death, or more precisely, death. People who are opposed to abortion see abortion as a form of killing. And euthanasia is, of course, about assisting someone to die. I will start with abortion.

METAPHYSICS

The issue here is complex as each side sees the issue in very different terms. They even refer to each other in different terms. The pro-choice side on the abortion debate calls the other side antichoice. On the other side the antichoice people call themselves pro life and see the pro-choice people as baby killers.

The pro-choice side sees the issue in terms of women having the right to control their own fertility. For too long, women's fertility was controlled by men in a patriarchal society. As women started to demand equal rights, control of their fertility was always in the forefront. A side issue was how women's sexuality was perceived. The two issues, while separate, are connected. This approach, of linking general questions about sexuality to questions about abortion and fertility, can be seen as using a feminist approach to the issue.

The pro-life side sees abortion as the killing of the fetus, which they see as an actual child. A slogan that is popular on their side is, " Life is sacred from conception to natural death." Thus the pro-life people see the two issues of abortion and euthanasia in the same light. In neither case should there be human interference.

Another way of putting the disagreement between the two views is whether the status of the fetus is morally relevant to the debate. The pro-choice side says no while the right to life side says yes.

Thus, in a very real sense, the debate over abortion is really two different debates. These differences can involve different approaches to morality from a secular perspective and from a religious perspective. The main thrust of this book is from a secular standpoint, but many people see religion as the basis of moral teaching. As we see in this section, religious teaching on the issue is divided, as is a secular approach.

Abortion Issues in the United States

More than four decades after the U.S. Supreme Court's Roe v. Wade decision, opponents and supporters of abortion rights are still battling over the issue in court, at the ballot box and in state legislatures. A recently enacted Alabama law has been described as the nation's most restrictive, and several other states also have passed new restrictions on abortion with an eye toward giving the Supreme Court a chance to overturn its decision in Roe.

As the debate over abortion continues, here are five key facts about Americans' views on the topic, based on recent Pew Research Center polling:

About six-in-ten U.S. adults (61 percent) said in a 2019 survey that abortion should be legal in all or most cases, compared with 38 percent who said it should be illegal all or most of the time. On both sides of the issue, Americans are more likely than not to leave room for exceptions, with more saying abortion should be legal or illegal *most* of the time, rather than always. Public support for legal abortion remains as high as it has been in two decades of polling, and there is virtually no difference between the views of men and women.

There is a substantial—and growing—partisan divide on abortion, with Democrats and those who lean toward the Democratic Party much more likely than Republicans and GOP leaners to support legal abortion in all or most cases (82 percent vs. 36 percent). There also are large gaps based on religious affiliation. For example, three-quarters of white evangelical Protestants (77 percent) say abortion should be illegal in all or most cases, while an even larger share of religiously unaffiliated Americans (83 percent) take the opposing view, saying that abortion should be mostly or entirely legal.[1]

The Christian position, specifically Roman Catholic, is presented as follows:

The Fifth Commandment
You shall not kill.

Human life is sacred because from its beginning it involves the creative action of God and it remains for ever in a special relationship with the Creator, who is its sole end. God alone is the Lord of life from its beginning until its end: no one can under any circumstance claim for himself the right directly to destroy an innocent human being.

The covenant between God and mankind is interwoven with reminders of God's gift of human life and man's murderous violence:

For your lifeblood I will surely require a reckoning. . . Whoever sheds the blood of man, by man shall his blood be shed; for God made man in his own image.

The Old Testament always considered blood a sacred sign of life. This teaching remains necessary for all time.[2]

Human life must be respected and protected absolutely from the moment of conception. From the first moment of his existence, a human being must be recognized as having the rights of a person - among which is the inviolable right of every innocent being to life.

The inalienable rights of the person must be recognized and respected by civil society and the political authority. These human rights depend neither on single individuals nor on parents; nor do they represent a concession made by society and the state; they belong to human nature and are inherent in the person by virtue of the creative act from which the person took his origin. Among such fundamental rights one should mention in this regard every human being's right to life and physical integrity from the moment of conception until death.

But there are Catholics who disagree. Catholics for Choice states on its website:

At CFC, we strive to be an expression of Catholicism as it is lived by ordinary people. We are part of the great majority of the faithful in the Catholic Church who disagrees with the dictates of the Vatican on matters related to sex, marriage, family life and motherhood. We are part of the great majority who believes that Catholic teachings on conscience mean that every individual must follow his or her own conscience—and respect others' rights to do the same. At Catholics for Choice we believe that this is the world where the meaning of choice can truly be realized. We believe that change happens through dialogue and an exchange of information, through communicating ideas and values.

We believe that change happens when we take courageous and strategic risks.

We know that change happens when we challenge well-established and unquestioned authority and enable people to hear new ideas and embrace new ways of thinking.

On issues of; Abortion and Contraception, HIV & AIDs, Sex and Sexuality, New Reproductive Technologies, Religion in Public Policy.

On all these issues Catholics for Choice provides effective counterpoint to the vocal, well-financed and powerful Roman Catholic hierarchy, which presents itself as the sole moral arbiter on matters where sexuality and reproduction intersect with religion and faith. We work to strengthen our partners' and colleagues' efforts by sharing our skills and learning from each other; successes and limitations. CFC is the only organization with the knowledge, expertise, strategic sense and courage to meet the very real threats resulting from the inappropriate role the Vatican tries to play in public policy.

Catholics for Choice seeks to engage all sectors of culture and society in ways that are meaningful to each. We strive to represent the voice and vision of Catholics and change the tone of the debate on reproductive rights.

Catholics for Choice seeks to shape and advance sexual and reproductive ethics that are based on justice, reflect a commitment to women's well-being and respect and affirm the capacity of women and men to make moral decisions about their lives. CFC works in the United States and internationally to ensure that all people have access to safe and affordable reproductive healthcare and services and to infuse our core values into public policy, community life and Catholic social thinking and teaching.[3]

And on the secular side.

The Canadian Association for the Repeal of the Abortion Laws (CARAL) was founded in November 1974 by pro-choice activists. CARAL changed its name to the Canadian Abortion Rights Action League in 1980.

CARAL played a leading role in the fight for women's right to a safe, legal abortion and better access to birth control. It developed widespread support for challenging the 1969 abortion law which allowed abortions only with the approval of a hospital Therapeutic Abortion Committee. Actions included demonstrations, public meetings, lobbying the government, and letter-writing campaigns. CARAL also backed Dr. Henry Morgentaler's legal challenges to the abortion law.

> The purpose of CARAL, as defined in its constitution, "is to ensure that no woman in Canada is denied access to safe, legal abortion." Its aim is "the repeal of all sections of the Criminal Code dealing with abortion, and the establishment of comprehensive contraceptive and abortion services, including appropriate counselling across the country." Removal of abortion from the Criminal Code "would permit all Canadians to act according to personal conscience." It would eliminate the current situation, in which Canada's Abortion Law is "unfairly and unequally applied and tends to discriminate against low income and rural women." Only one-fifth of Canadian Hospitals have Therapeutic Abortion Committees; yet a Gallup poll done in June 1982 "showed that 72 percent of

adult Canadians believe that the decision whether or not to have abortion should rest with the consenting patient."

CARAL maintains an extensive file on abortion around the world, and publishes a bibliography and information materials. (One article, entitled "When Does Life Begin?—The Evolving Position of the Roman Catholic Church," traces the history of the church's position on abortion.) Members are also active in lobbying politicians across the country.

CARAL points out that it is not pro-abortion, but that they do recognize that "all birth control methods can fail, and unwanted pregnancies do occur. . . it's a situation where there are no good answers, only rational decisions." "In a humane and caring society, every child should be a wanted child." This organization no longer exists.[4]

And from a medical standpoint,

The CMA's position on induced abortion is as follows: Induced abortion is the active termination of a pregnancy before fetal viability. The decision to perform an induced abortion is a medical one, made confidentially between the patient and her physician within the confines of existing Canadian law. The decision is made after conscientious examination of all other options. Induced abortion requires medical and surgical expertise and is a medical act. It should be performed only in a facility that meets approved medical standards, not necessarily a hospital. Induced abortion, as interpreted by the CMA, is the active termination of a pregnancy before fetal viability. In this context viability is the ability of the fetus to survive independently of the maternal environment. According to current medical knowledge viability is dependent on fetal weight, degree of development and length of gestation; extrauterine viability may be possible if the fetus weighs over five hundred g or is past twenty weeks' gestation, or both (Gestation begins at conception). In January 1988 the Supreme Court of Canada struck down section 251 of the Criminal Code of Canada. The CMA's position is that there is no need for this section to be replaced. The following are the CMA's positions in other matters related to induced abortion. Induced abortion should not be used as an alternative to contraception. Counselling services, family planning services and information on contraception must be readily available to all Canadians. The provision of advice and information on family planning and human sexuality is the responsibility of practising physicians; however, educational institutes and health care agencies must share this responsibility. The patient should be provided with the option of full and immediate counselling services in the event of unwanted pregnancy. Since the risks of complications of induced abortion are lowest in early pregnancy,[5]

And from a biological standpoint.

There is no sharp limit of development, gestational age, or weight at which a human fetus automatically becomes viable.[1] According to studies between 2003 and 2005, twenty to 35 percent of babies born at 23 weeks of gestation survive, while fifty to seventy percent of babies born at 24 to 25 weeks, and more than ninety percent born at 26 to 27 weeks, survive .[4] It is rare for a baby weighing less than five hundred g (17.6 ounces) to survive. [1] A baby's chances for survival increase three to four percent per day between 23 and 24 weeks of gestation and about two to three percent per day between 24 and 26 weeks of gestation. After 26 weeks the rate of survival increases at a much slower rate because survival is high already.

EPISTEMOLOGY

Here we have to look at the evidence regarding the opposing claims. Since the pro-choice side does not see the status of the fetus as morally relevant, at least to some extent, while the right to life side does, if we can get a clear sense of fetal development which can be applied to the question, that would help in resolving the debate.

VALUES

Here the values of each side will be assessed. Values come from communities and have a factual component, as we have seen. So the arguments on both sides will be evaluated. We will also evaluate motive and intents and look at possible consequences of decisions.

LOGIC

Reasoning will be used to see if there can be a resolution to the debate.

DISCUSSION

I would like to start the discussion on an anthropological note. Historically, when faced with an overpopulation situation, many groups would practice infanticide, and it was almost always the girl infants who were killed, as a means of not only controlling population at the moment but also for the future, since it is girls who grow into women who give birth. As Marvin Harris points out that small bands, unlike state societies,

> Were exceptional in their use of warfare to achieve very low rates of population growth. They achieved this not primarily through male combat deaths—which

... are always easily compensated for by calling upon the remarkable reproductive reserves of the human female—but by another means that was not part of the actual fighting. I refer to female infanticide. Warfare in band and village societies made the practice of infanticide sex-specific. It encouraged the rearing of sons, whose masculinity was glorified in preparation for combat, and the devaluation of daughters who did not fight. This in turn led to the limitation of female children by neglect, abuse, and outright infanticide.[6]

He goes on to say,

I am not suggesting that war caused female infanticide or that the practice of female infanticide caused war. Rather, I propose that without reproductive pressure neither warfare nor female infanticide would have been widespread and that the conjunction of the two represents a savage but uniquely effective solution to a Malthusian dilemma.[7]

Some of these points are developed by anthropologist Laila Williamson, who points out that infanticide is very widespread, both culturally and historically. Virtually every society has practiced it in one form or another. The primary reason is population control and an adjustment to environmental and economic resources. She goes on to point out that infanticide is often employed when abortion techniques are either ineffective or non-existent.[8]

Williamson makes an important point regarding the value of life where "killing a newborn is often explained as a caring act, done to save the life of an older sibling who is too young to be weaned."[9] And she finally concludes, largely in agreement with Harris, that "(T)he adjustment to food resources, to the subsistence pattern of each society, or to nomadic conditions appear to be very basic reasons for infanticide, as it was the only practical and reliable method for limiting the number of children."[10]

While I certainly do not want to imply that abortion is a means of population control, I point this out to make the connection between how women are perceived as carriers of future generations and not as persons in their own right. Looking at women in this way supports the view that the role of women is to be mothers. But as the women's movement has developed over the last three quarters of a century or so, this notion is being challenged. Women are persons and as such can function on their own in the world. They do not have to be mothers. They can have careers of their own. They need to be in control of their fertility, which is why abortion rights are so important to women. For, without that control, without that right, women cannot become fully functional moral persons.

Thus, from this perspective, the pro-choice side has nothing to do with the fetus and everything to do with the status of women. If women are to become truly equal they must have the right to decide what to do with their bodies.

To put this point differently in this context, the right to abortion is necessary for gender equality.

In other words, women are full-fledged people with full moral standing and must be in control of their reproductive processes. If a society says that women cannot terminate pregnancies, then women are reduced to something less than full standing moral members of society. Thus the right to abortion is a moral issue with regards the status of women. And, from this perspective, to deny the right to abortion would be considered immoral, for it denies moral status to women.

Now, much of the discussion on abortion revolves around the status of the fetus. As we see from a medical standpoint, if we discuss the notion of viability, then the fetus becomes morally relevant when its cognitive functions start to develop, well into the late part of the second trimester, and into the third trimester. Thus a pro-choice person can acknowledge the moral relevancy of the fetus at this time, but not before.

And, as many jurisdictions have laws regarding the nature of personhood, it usually is with birth. Before that a fetus is not considered a person.

But, as we have seen above, the fetus is morally relevant for the right to life side. So the pro-choice side tries to answer the right to life side by arguing that even if the fetus is a person, there are times when abortion is still permissible.

In a very interesting article on the subject Judith Jarvis Thomson argues this point.

> She sets up analogies where people are forced to do things they would not want to do—one is being hooked up to another person whose kidneys are failing in order to keep that person alive. But the question is, why should one person sacrifice a life for another? Thus it is permissible for the forced donor to say no. That is, a pregnant woman can say no to the pregnancy. She need not be in that situation against her will.[11]

There is a lot of discussion also on the nature of killing. The big argument against abortion is that it is killing a person. But there are all types of situations where our society condones killing, from self-defense to war. Thus, under certain circumstances, abortion would be permissible under analogous situations such as if the pregnancy is endangering the mother's life.

Right to life people also acknowledge the possibility of abortion in cases of rape. Which means that, at least to some extent, they recognize the value of the woman as a person and not just as a carrier of a potential person. While I mention this point, I do not want to belabor it and push it to extremes. But is important to mention.

Then there is the argument that pro-life people use in talking about the fetus as a potential person. The fallacy here is that to compare a fetus to a potential person is to compare an acorn to a potential oak tree. The acorn may blossom into an oak tree, but it can also be eaten by a squirrel. An acorn is not a tree.

But to continue the discussion, I turn to the work of Mary Ann Warren. She picks up on this last point and argues that

> ... advocates of a right to choose abortion point to the terrible consequences of prohibiting it, especially while contraception is still unreliable, and is financially beyond the reach of much of the world's population. Worldwide, hundreds of thousands of women die each year from illegal abortions, and many more suffer from complications that may leave them injured or infertile. Women who are poor, underage, disabled, or otherwise vulnerable, suffer from the absence of safe and legal abortion. Advocates of abortion also argue that to deny a woman access to abortion is to deprive her of the right to control her own body—a right so fundamental that without it other rights are often all but meaningless.[12]

She acknowledges that these arguments do not convince abortion opponents because of their fundamental belief in the status of the fetus. In this context she raises the question regarding the status of the fetus as a person. And she refers to Thomson's argument that from a moral standpoint, women are not obliged to complete an unwanted pregnancy.[13]

In developing the moral concept of what characteristics entitle an entity to be considered a person she outlines the following six:

1. Sentience—the capacity to have conscious experiences;
2. Emotionality—the capacity to feel, happy, sad, and so on;
3. Reason—the capacity to solve new and relatively complex problems;
4. The capacity to communicate—by whatever means, messages of an indefinite variety of topics;
5. Self-awareness—having a concept of oneself;
6. Moral agency—the capacity to regulate one's own actions[14]

She then applies these to the fetus and to animals and concludes that a "fetus does not resemble a person in ways which support the claim that it has strong moral rights." And she concludes that "fetuses are neither persons nor members of a moral community. Furthermore, neither a fetus's resemblance to a person, nor its potential for becoming a person, provides an adequate basis for the claim that it has a full and equal right to life."[15]

Now these pro-choice arguments have, of course, been responded to. The main argument against the pro-choice position is, of course, the standing of the fetus. Don Marquis argues, in response to Thomson that "an opponent of abortion might point out that a women's right to use her own body does not entail her right to end someone else's life in order to do what she wants with her body." Marquis continues that the fetus deserves a "future like ours."[16]

Marquis goes on to argue against the various views where a life can be taken, from abortion to euthanasia. And in all cases he argues that since murder is wrong, taking a life, which would prevent that life from having a future like ours would be immoral.

Marquis's whole argument, as clever as it is, is based on the view that taking life is wrong and that a fetus is a life.

But this question of future life raises another issue: What happens to a baby who is born to a mother who does not want the baby, or is in no position to look after a child, which is why she wanted the abortion in the first place? Do the right to life people step up and adopt the baby? Or does some form of social services take over?

If anti choice people are really concerned about babies having a future life, one would think they also would have an obligation to see that the baby gets that future life.

CONCLUSIONS

Metaphysics

As we have seen, the two sides see the issue completely differently. So, in one sense there is no resolution. The one common area, if it can be called that, is in the later stages of pregnancy, where even the pro-choice people acknowledge there should be no late abortions since the fetus is probably viable, and an abortion at such a late stage may pose a health risk to the mother. On the other side of the issue, a late abortion may be called for if the mother's life is endangered by the continued pregnancy.

A good example of this can be found in Peter Kreet's book, *Three Approaches to Abortion*. The last section is a fictional debate between "Libby, the pro-choicer, is a 'sassy, classy, Black feminist' and Isa, the pro-lifer is a 'Muslim fundamentalist philosopher."[17] To Kreet's credit he portrays both sides fairly and has them at a complete impasse, for the reasons given above.

But perhaps one way to get around this impasse is to ask women, especially younger women, who have abortions out of necessity, but didn't really want to have them, to discuss their reasoning and emotional reactions. By talking to women who went through the process, but who didn't want to, but for their own reasons felt they had to, we might get a more complete view of the issue, especially from people who have been there.

Epistemology

The only real facts in the issue are the medical facts about fetal development. While in some sense life begins at conception, it is not yet a human life. As the medical data shows, a fetus becomes viable at around the onset of the third trimester. In most developed societies, laws state that the fetus becomes a person at birth. But, one could argue that a viable fetus is close to becoming that person.

If one looks at teen pregnancy rates in the United States one sees that the rates are significantly higher in places where abstention is taught and proper sex education is not taught. So by educating teens about sex pregnancy rates actually go down. And if unwanted pregnancy rates go down, so will abortions.[18]

Values

We can look at the two sides of this issue as two different cultures, each with their own sets of values regarding the status of women and the status of the fetus. There are two groups of people living in the same physical communities but who represent different cultural communities. So we have to apply what we learned in our discussion of multiculturism. Both groups have to learn to live with the other. While there can be discussion and logical debate to try to influence the thinking of the other group, there can be no coercion, no outright hostility, no threat to life.

If we look at the motives behind the need for abortion we most often find that the pregnancy is unwanted. Sometimes it because of rape, sometimes it is because of failed birth control and sometimes no real thought went into the cause. But the point pro-choice women make is that the reason the woman got pregnant is not the issue. The issue is having control over the situation.

In terms of consequences, there are two points to be made. One has to do with the situation of a woman who is pregnant but is in no position to maintain the pregnancy or to care for a child. If she is forced to carry the fetus to term there will be psychological damage done to her. The second point is that there can be serious repercussions for the child, especially if the child cannot be properly looked after.

As a follow up, a new study done by Corinne Rocca at the University of California, San Francisco surveyed 667 women who had abortions across 21 states that have a variety of laws. They were first interviewed about a week after the abortion and then were interviewed semi-annually for up to five years. "About half the women said that decision to have an abortion had been a difficult one at the time, but five years later 99 percent said it had been the right one."[19]

Logic

Each side presents a case based on a set of values. We can acknowledge that given the respective premises, each side argues validly for its respective position.

So again, culture, or a set of cultural values, trumps logic since neither side will acknowledge the starting point of the other.

EUTHANASIA

The term euthanasia literally means "a good death," from the Greek. "Eu" in Greek means "good" and "thanatos" means "death." The idea behind the concept is that people should be in control of how they die. It is usually discussed in terms of ending suffering, especially in the case of a terminal illness.

METAPHYSICS

On one side of the issue we have people saying that we should be in control of our own lives.

Proponents of euthanasia and physician-assisted suicide (PAS) contend that terminally ill people should have the right to end their suffering with a quick, dignified, and compassionate death. They argue that the right to die is protected by the same constitutional safeguards that guarantee such rights as marriage, procreation, and the refusal or termination of life-saving medical treatment.[20]

While on the other side people say that taking a life, regardless of the situation is wrong. This side has people on both secular and religious views.

To quote from the same site:

> Opponents of euthanasia and physician-assisted suicide contend that doctors have a moral responsibility to keep their patients alive as reflected in the Hippocratic Oath. They argue there may be a "slippery slope" from euthanasia to murder, and that legalizing euthanasia will unfairly target the poor and disabled and create incentives for insurance companies to terminate lives in order to save money.

Two points are raised here, the obligations of doctors, who are healers, and, if it can be put this way, the effects of profit-making capitalism in health decision making.

Issues of Life and Death 91

The capitalism issue was discussed at length in chapter one where it was argued that capitalism, to properly function, must be controlled by community values. That is the economy must serve the community. Thus, if life is valued, and health care is provided, insurance companies, whether private or public, will be controlled in how their decisions are made. Profit at the expense of life would not be permitted on that model.

The second issue has to deal with the notion of care. One way of talking about euthanasia has been to use the term "mercy killing." Thus, while doctors do try to preserve life, they can also provide mercy to alleviate suffering.

EPISTEMOLOGY

Here we will look at how personhood is understood and the information about who or what we are, especially with regard to brain functions and our conception of life.

The following information is from the website of the Government of the Netherlands.

Euthanasia, Assisted Suicide and Non-Resuscitation on Request
Euthanasia is performed by the attending physician administering a fatal dose of a suitable drug to the patient on his or her express request. The relevant Dutch legislation also covers physician-assisted suicide (where the physician supplies the drug but the patient administers it). Palliative sedation is not a form of euthanasia: the patient is simply rendered unconscious with pain reducing drugs and eventually dies from natural causes.

What the Law Says
Euthanasia and assisted suicide are legal only if the criteria laid down in the Dutch termination of Life on Request and Assisted Suicide (Review Procedures) Act are fully observed. Only then is the physician concerned immune from criminal prosecution. Requests for euthanasia often come from patients experiencing unbearable suffering with no prospect of improvement. Their request must be made earnestly and with full conviction. They see euthanasia as the only escape from the situation. However, patients have no absolute right to euthanasia and doctors no absolute duty to perform it.

Guidelines for Euthanasia of Semi-Conscious Patients
Sometimes, a patient may lapse into semi-consciousness just before a scheduled euthanasia. If there are still signs of suffering, the doctor may perform euthanasia despite the patient's lowered consciousness. This is laid down in guidelines on the subject prepared by the Royal Dutch Medical Association at

the request of the Board of Procurators General of the Public Prosecution Office and the Healthcare Inspectorate. These guidelines on euthanasia of patients with lowered consciousness do not represent any implicit relaxation of the law; they are merely designed to provide guidance for physicians in this difficult situation.

Advance Directives

Some people feel that they would wish euthanasia to be performed if they ever find themselves in a particular situation which they would now regard as unbearable and offering no prospect of improvement. Their best course of action is to discuss the situation they envisage with their family doctor and make a written directive covering those circumstances. Such advance directives define the precise circumstances in which the patients concerned would wish euthanasia to be performed. The document constitutes a request to the physician and must contain a clear and unambiguous expression of the patient's wishes.

Euthanasia and Assisted Suicide

Termination of life on request can take two forms. In the case of euthanasia, the physician administers a fatal dose of a suitable drug to the patient. In assisted suicide, by contrast, the physician supplies the lethal drug but the patient administers it. Both forms are covered by the Act and in both cases doctors must fulfil the statutory due care criteria. Every instance of euthanasia and assisted suicide must be reported to one of the five regional euthanasia review committees. The committee will judge if the physician has taken due care. If a physician fails to do so, he may be prosecuted. Penalties vary but may be as much as 12 years in prison for euthanasia and up to three years for assisting suicide.

Euthanasia and Minors

Minors may themselves request euthanasia from the age of 12, although the consent of the parents or guardian is mandatory until they reach the age of 16. Sixteen and seventeen-year-olds do not need parental consent in principle, but their parents must be involved in the decision-making process. From the age of 18, young people have the right to request euthanasia without parental involvement.

Euthanasia and Patients with Dementia

For some people, the prospect of ever suffering from dementia may be sufficient reason to make an advance directive (living will). This can either be drawn up independently or discussed first with the family doctor. A physician can perform euthanasia on a patient with dementia only if such a directive exists, if statutory care is taken and if, in his opinion, the patient is experiencing unbearable suffering with no prospect of improvement.

Review Committee

Doctors have a duty to report all unnatural deaths to the municipal pathologist. In cases of euthanasia, the latter then notifies a regional review committee.

Such committees comprise, at the minimum, a medical doctor, an ethicist and a legal expert. The committee assesses whether the physician who performed the euthanasia has fulfilled the statutory due care criteria. The review committee procedure is intended to ensure greater transparency and consistency in the way cases are reported and assessed.

The procedure benefits both the Public Prosecution Service and physicians. The statutory criteria and the findings of the review committees tell doctors how their actions in particular cases are likely to stand up to legal, medical and ethical scrutiny.

This shows that there need be no worries regarding the slippery slope as long as the strict criteria are followed. Which, according to data from Holland, is shown to be the case.[21]

Canada has recently passed a similar law. The Government of Canada has launched an online public consultation aimed at obtaining Canadian's views on amending the federal Medical Assistance in Dying legislation. Canadians and interested stakeholders were invited to share their views online until January 27, 2020.

Changes to the Criminal Code

In February 2015, the Supreme Court of Canada ruled in Carter v. Canada that parts of the Criminal Code would need to change to satisfy the Canadian Charter of Rights and Freedoms. The parts that prohibited medical assistance in dying would no longer be valid. The Supreme Court gave the government until June 6, 2016, to create a new law.

In June 2016, the Parliament of Canada passed federal legislation that allows eligible Canadian adults to request medical assistance in dying.

Who can provide medical assistance in dying and who can help?

Those who can provide medical assistance in dying services are:

- physicians
- nurse practitioners (in provinces where this is allowed)

Those who can help provide medical assistance in dying include:

- pharmacists
- family members or other people that you ask to help
- health care providers who help physicians or nurse practitioners

These people can assist in the process without being charged under criminal law. However, physicians, nurse practitioners and other people who are directly involved must follow:

- the rules set out in the Criminal Code
- applicable provincial and territorial health-related laws, rules and policies

Protecting the Right of Providers to Act According to Their Beliefs and Values

Not all health care providers will be comfortable with medical assistance in dying. The federal practice may not be consistent with a provider's beliefs and values. The federal legislation does not force any person to provide or help to provide medical assistance in dying.

Provincial and territorial governments have the responsibility for determining how and where health care services are provided. They may also make policies around where medical assistance in dying can take place as long as they do not conflict with the Criminal Code.

Supporting access for patients seeking medical assistance in dying

We understand that these provider rights could create problems for patients who want to access medical assistance in dying. Most provinces and territories have developed care coordination systems to help patients learn more about this service.[22]

VALUES

Here we look at how we value life, or what it means to be alive. If a person is in a vegetative state, what do we do? We look at intent and consequences.

Some of the questions regarding this issue are: Is it ever permissible to take a life, and if so, under what conditions would it be permissible? Is there is a difference between actively ending someone's life or letting that person die by withdrawing treatment?

LOGIC

Making connections between our conception of life and death, our values and our knowledge of life and death.

DISCUSSION

I would like to begin the discussion by tying it to the discussion above regarding infanticide.

As Joseph Fletcher argues, "what is good and right for a person when he does it for himself, e.g., suicide, is just as good and right, and for the same reasons, when it is done for him by proxy (i.e., allocide). Thus, on this view assisted death would be completely acceptable.[23]

Thus, if we accept suicide as acceptable, we should allow someone else to aid in a suicide. This was a theme of the 1969 movie, *They Shoot Horses, Don't They*? which was based on a 1930s novel by Horace McCoy. The question becomes if I want to die but am incapable of doing it myself, why can't I get someone to assist me?

The issue of euthanasia or assisted suicide is all about ending suffering. If someone is in terrible pain and there is no cure for their condition, and if the person is considered terminal, then why should we not be able to hasten their death to avoid unnecessary suffering? Proponents of euthanasia are very careful to avoid the "slippery slope" argument put forward by opponents. Proponents would want very strict criteria for allowing euthanasia since they would not want to cause unnecessary harm or death to anyone.

The issue is discussed in two very different situations. The first, hinted at above, is when someone is suffering, and is terminal, or at least near terminal—the person is going to die soon—so why let them suffer?

The second situation is when someone is on life support systems. The question becomes, will the person be able to function on their own if taken off life support?

This case raises the issue of definition of death. For most of our history, death was defined in respiratory terms: if one is not breathing, or if one's heart has stopped, one is dead. But with developments in medicine and technology this is no longer the case. We can resuscitate a stopped heart in a number of ways, from performing basic first aid to using mechanical means, to using drugs. Sometimes, a combination of techniques is required. The important point here is that while the respiratory definition of death is valid in many cases, it does not always apply, especially in cases of people on life support systems.

This is also in part because of developments in neurology and in changing our definition of what is it is to be a person.

So what do we replace it with? The answer is in some sense one of brain functions. There is the whole or total brain view and the upper functions view. The total brain view is that if there is no brain activity at all, or if the brain damage is irreversible, we can say the person is dead. The higher brain function view is that a person can be declared dead if the higher functions of the brain, those controlling thought, speech and memory, are not functioning. For all practical reasons, the person is no longer a person, and is therefore dead. In such cases we can take a person off a life support system.

Most textbooks on bio-ethics, where these issues are raised, have some kind of case study to base discussions on. Such a case study would include a person on life support, for any number of reasons: a bad allergic reaction, a drug overdose, a car accident, and so on. An EEG is performed and, while there is some brain activity, most of the higher functions are not there. Because some function shows up there is a disagreement as to whether the person is alive or not. Further complicating the issue is when the parents or next of kin are religious and opposed to taking the person off life support unless it can be conclusively shown the person is truly brain dead.

So a discussion between the doctors and the family begins. Clearly, because of differing views on life and death, and also differing values regarding making decisions about life and death, there is no clear-cut answer. But of course the purpose of such an illustration is to develop debate and to get students to work things through for themselves.

One issue I raised above has to do with the distinction between active and passive euthanasia. Active euthanasia means that some action will be taken to end a person's life. But for people who sympathize with the notion of euthanasia but cannot bring themselves to act on it, have argued for the notion of passive euthanasia, which amounts to letting the patient die without intervention, or by medical omission, that is not doing a treatment or procedure to keep the patient alive.

The main argument against passive euthanasia is that it may prolong suffering and thereby cause more pain and more harm to the patient in question. This used to be a major topic of debate, but since various countries have brought in so-called right to die laws, the views on passive euthanasia are no longer in the forefront of the discussion.

CONCLUSIONS

Metaphysics

Again, as with abortion, the two opposing sides do not meet. People who are opposed to any taking of life will not be persuaded by logical arguments in favor of some version of euthanasia, nor will they be swayed by empirical data regarded no exploitation of such a practice.

People in favor of some form of euthanasia try to meet objections by pointing to evidence and of the moral need for having access to such practices.

Epistemology

As we have seen from Holland, and now in Canada, where such laws exist, the criteria are very strict and there is no evidence of allowing assisted death leading to the slippery slope of allowing all kinds of people to be euthanized.

Values

Here we see a true clash of values, where one side values the notion of life so much they will not allow any taking of life. On religious grounds the argument is that only God can take a life and people cannot play God. But even on the secular side, the argument is essentially the same: we cannot take a life. Regardless of the circumstances, it is still murder.

For people who are in favor of some version of euthanasia the moral argument—the intent—is to alleviate unnecessary suffering, especially in the case of a terminal illness. The alleviating of suffering is seen to be moral and can therefore justify the taking of a life. The consequences of not taking the life can be extreme unnecessary suffering.

One more point should be mentioned here. Part of the dispute has to do with new knowledge and new technologies challenging old values. Many people still hold to the respiratory view of life and death, while, as we have seen above, advances in medical science, such as respirators and new medications, have changed the definition life and death to brain functions. Here we have another clash of values, but this clash, hopefully can be resolved by looking at the facts in question.

Logic

Again we see how belief systems or value systems held rigidly do not allow for logical or evidential arguments to change one's views. Thus culture or value structures override logic.

NOTES

1. "5 Facts About the Abortion Debate in America," Fact Tank, Pew Research, August 30, 2019, https://www.pewresearch/fact-tank/2019/08/30/facts-about-abortion-in-america. Site checked July 31, 2020.

2. "Catechism of the Catholic Church," The Vatican, https://www.Vatican.va/archive/ccc_css/archive/catechism/p3s2 c2a5.htm. Site checked July 31.2020.

3. "About our Work", Catholics for Choice, https://www.catholicsforchoice.org/about-us/about-our-work. Site checked July 31, 2020.

4. "Canadian Abortion Rights Action League (CARAL)," Rise Up! A Digital Archive of Feminist Activism, Digitizing Feminist Activism, https://www.riseupfeministarchive.ca/activism/organizations/canadian-abortion-rights-action-league-caral. Site checked July 31, 2020.

5. Canadian Medical Association Policy on Induced Abortion, Canadian Medical Association, December 1988, https://www.personhood.ca/pdfs/cma_policy.pdf. Site checked July 31, 2020

6. Harris, Marvin, *Cannibals and Kings*, 49.

7. Harris 51

8. Williamson, Linda, "Infanticide: An Anthropological Analysis" in *Marvin Kohl, Infanticide and the value of Life* 61–63.

9. Williamson, 63

10. Williamson, 73

11. Thomson, Judith Jarvis, "A Defense of Abortion," in Lafollette.

12. Warren, Mary Ann, "On the Moral and Legal Status of Abortion," in Lafollette ed. Ethics in Practice: An Anthology, 4 ed. (Oxford: Wiley and Sons, 2014) 132.

13. Williamson, 133.

14. Williamson, 136.

15. Williamson, 138–140.

16. Marquis Don, An argument that Abortion is Wrong, in Lafollette 142.

17. Kreet, Peter, *Three Approaches to Abortion*, (San Francisco: Ignatius Press 2002) 73.

18. "Teen Birth Rate by State," National Center for Health Statistics, Centers for Disease Control and Prevention. https://www.cdc.gov/nchs/pressroom/sosmap/teen-births/teenbirths.htm. Site checked July 31, 2020.

19. Rocca, Corrinne, *New Scientist*, 18 January 2020.

20. "Should Euthanasia or Physician-Assisted Suicide be Legal?" Britannica Pro-Con, https://www.euthanasia.procon.org. Site checked July 31.2020.

21. "Euthanasia, Assisted Suicide and Non-Resuscitation on Request," Government of the Netherlands, https://www.government.nl/topics/euthanasia/euthanasia-assisted-suicide-and-non-resuscitation-on-request. Site checked July 31.2020.

22. "Medical Assistance in Dying," Health Canada, Government of Canada, https://www.canada.ca/en/health-canada-services/medical-assistance-dying. Site checked July 31.2020.

23. Fletcher, Joseph, "Infanticide and the Ethics of Loving Concern," in Kohl.

Chapter Five

Slavery, Human Trafficking and Prostitution

Putting these three issues together may seem strange but many people see human trafficking as a form of slavery. That is, the purpose of trafficking is to sell a person into some form of servitude, very often sexual. And many people see prostitution as a form of servitude. So the linkage makes sense. But, of course, not everyone sees these linkages, therefore we will look at the three issues both separately and together.

METAPHYSICS

First we will look at slavery, which is defined in various ways, including servitude, subjugation, serfdom, bondage and restricted freedom. To put it starkly, a slave is the property of someone else. Slaves are not seen as persons but as property.

Human trafficking is the buying and selling of persons, all too often for sexual reasons, but also for the purposes of mercenary work and other forms of forced labor, as we saw in the American South where slaves did the hard work on plantations but also worked as house servants. That is often interpreted as people being sold into prostitution, which is why some critics of prostitution see it as a form of slavery, where people are forced to work in the sex trades, and are, more often than not, not in control of their own bodies.

EPISTEMOLOGY

Here we look at actual practices. Part of that will be to listen to people in various situations such as those working in the sex trades. But first a little history of slavery.

Slavery has been a part of human history since the beginnings of civilization. As reddit.com points out slavery was rarely found in hunter gather societies because it usually develops along with social stratification, where there is a large enough population and an economic surplus. Slavery was also used as a form of punishment and for prisoners of war. It existed in ancient societies such as Sumer, which dates to 3500 BCE and is mentioned in the code of Hammurabi C 1860 BCE. We also know of slavery from the Old Testament. The time of Moses was circa 1500 BCE. And slavery was practiced in Ancient Greece and Rome.

Slavery as such is outlawed today but still persists in small areas, especially in war regions. ISIS took slaves. But today it is the human trafficking issue that has become the main issue.

Prostitution also has a long history. As Nils Johan Ringdal points out, though it is not the world's oldest profession, it has been around a long time and is known to exist throughout parts of the ancient world.[1] He argues that "Although prostitution is neither universal nor found in all societies, the sex market has enjoyed formidable customer demand throughout history."[2] We know prostitution existed in the Ancient near east. The Ancient Near Eastwas home to many shrines, temples or "houses of heaven," which were dedicated to various deities. These shrines and temples were documented by the Greek historian Herodotus in The Histories,[4] where sacred prostitution was a common practice. Sumerian records dating back to ca. 2400 BCE are the earliest recorded mention of prostitution as an occupation.

Ringdal discusses the stories of prostitution in the Old Testament and also talks a great deal about the *Epic of Gilgamesh*, which dates from around 1800 BCE but most probably reflects stories that date back to about 2600 BCE. The epic describes the role of the goddess Ishtar "and the sexual assistance offered by women in and around her temples."[3] His point is that some form of prostitution was taking place. But here it was part of the religion. Family life was important, but fathers could decide if a daughter would get married or serve in a temple. "We hardly know what the women wanted or preferred. But it is likely that some thought themselves better off with a life in a temple."[4]

He also discusses the notion of dowries and bride prices. "While higher classes obtained brides with dowries, often including their personal slaves, those who had less, paid for their brides." The idea of a price for a bride was to compensate for her lost labor. He points out that the poor seldom provided dowries but could sell a daughter as a bride or as a slave or could send her to a temple. This point seems to separate slavery from prostitution and puts prostitution on a higher level. And Ringdal also points out that "Male prostitution seems to have just as old a link to temple rites and religious life as female, but to date, no one has managed to clarify this relationship fully."[5]

Human trafficking is defined as the trade in persons for the purposes of forced labor, sexual slavery or commercial exploitation, usually of a sexual nature. According to the International Labor Organization forced labor alone generates $150 billion annually as of 2014. And as of 2012 there were some 21 million victims trapped in modern-day slavery. Human trafficking is thought to be one of the fastest growing activities of trans-national crime organizations.[6]

VALUES

Slavery today is outlawed, although in various forms it is still practiced. To treat someone as a slave is to treat that person as less than one's moral equal. It is to treat another person as less than a person. Thus slavery is by definition, immoral.

So we must ask why someone would work as a slaver. The answer is usually economic benefit. One person makes money by selling another person into slavery—by treating that other person as a commodity instead of as a person. And the buyer will benefit from the free labor of the slave.

The article mentioned above points out that some 21 million people are trapped in modern day slavery. 14.2 million are exploited for labor, 4.5 million are sexually exploited, and the remainder are exploited in a state of forced labor.

While human trafficking is thought to be one of the fastest growing activities of transnational criminal organizations, it has been condemned as a violation of human rights by international conventions.

Vulnerable Groups

Trafficking in Persons Report released in June 2016 states that "refugees and migrants; lesbian, gay, bisexual, transgender, and intersex (LGBTI) individuals; religious minorities; people with disabilities; and those who are stateless" are the most at-risk for human trafficking. Governments best protect victims from being exploited when the needs of vulnerable populations are understood. Additionally, in its Protocol to Prevent, Suppress and Punish Trafficking in Persons, Especially Women and Children, the United Nations notes that women and children are particularly at risk for human trafficking and revictimization. The Protocol requires State Parties not only to enact measures that prevent human trafficking but also to address the factors that exacerbate women and children's vulnerability, including "poverty, underdevelopment and lack of equal opportunity."

Sexual trafficking includes coercing a migrant into a sexual act as a condition of allowing or arranging the migration. Sexual trafficking uses physical or sexual coercion, deception, abuse of power and bondage incurred through forced debt. Trafficked women and children, for instance, are often promised work in the domestic or service industry, but are instead sometimes taken to brothels where they are required to undertake sex work, while their passports and other identification papers are confiscated. They may be beaten or locked up and promised their freedom only after earning—through prostitution—their purchase price, as well as their travel and visa costs.

LOGIC

Here we will make connections. We will especially look at the notion of the sex trades in relation to human trafficking.

DISCUSSION

The discussion will pick up on the history of prostitution and we will also hear from people working in the sex trades.

Prostitution existed in different forms in Ancient Greece. Ringdal quotes Demosthenes on the subject: "Greek men of his day 'had h*etaerae* for their pleasure, concubines to care for their bodies and wives to secure the legitimacy of their descendants and keep their homes in order.'

He then goes on to say that "(T)he best-paid Greek prostitutes were, in many ways, the world's first free women. . . . They purchased their freedom, struggled for advancement, conquered literature and conditioned and coaxed their bodies to ultimate beauty. Their labors allowed them to advance socially, through better and more handsome men, than the cleverest princesses of the East."[7]

In the Hindu world the Vedic texts show that people were aware of prostitution. The Vedic word *sadharani* refers to a woman who offers sex for payment. And the Upanishads mention that sons of husbandless women and students quarreled with such women about payment. And, of course, there is the famous *Kama Sutra* which provided training for prostitutes.[8]

But the important civilization where much of our views on the subject come from is Rome, which was very patriarchal. In the temples of Venus, matrons could be promiscuous and counsel younger women. There would be both male and female prostitutes.

But the most important aspect of Roman views is that they separated sex from love. "One could have sex with anyone who aroused lust, as long as no man of rank, his wife, or his daughter was offended. While the Romans had a relaxed view of sex, they greatly feared love."[9] And as Ringdal points out male prostitution was never as widespread as in Rome.[10]

Things changed with the development of Christianity, but within the religion there were differences. Paul, who is very influential here, was influenced by the Greek Orphic's negative views on women, and as a result, argued for celibacy.[11] But there was also a cult of Mary which was much more sex positive. There is great discussion about who Mary Magdalene was. And there was confusion between Mary, Mother of Jesus, and Mary Magdalene. And in the Gospel of Mary, Jesus is quoted as saying "there is no sin in reality! It is you who create sin, when you do deeds such as adultery, which are called sin." The implication of this is that there is no original sin.

But the main views about sexuality came from St. Augustine, who would "defend prostitution as a bulwark against general immorality."[12] But celibacy was still held as the ideal.

But beginning in the 1300s and for the next century and a half or so popular literature started to poke fun at the Church. As Ringdal points out " (T)he late Middle Ages have been called a time without morals." He goes on to say that "(T)his characterization is apt, for prostitution enjoyed better conditions and was of greater extent than both before and after." Brothels existed from Naples to London, Nuremberg and Leipzig. The French words *borde*, *bordieau* and *bordlet* corresponded to the Italian bordello and were derived from the Saxon *borda*, meaning little house.[13]

The next important development in the history of prostitution was the discovery of syphilis. The term comes from the name of a Haitian shepherd of that name who is the hero of a 1530 poem by Giolamo Facastoro, a Veronese doctor. The term venereal disease comes from the goddess Venus. And as early as 1495 the Emperor Maximilian of Habsburg decreed that the illness was the result of common immorality, and most people attributed the spread of the disease to prostitutes. This factor, in the context of the Protestant reformation led to a stronger struggle against prostitution, and by the end of the sixteenth century prostitution "had fallen into a state of ill repute. . ."[14]

In the sixteenth and seventeenth centuries the courtesan appeared. Renaissance writers made sharp distinctions between prostitutes and courtesans. "A courtesan was richly attired, lived respectably, and would scarcely be seen at a public bath or in a brothel. She preferred to receive at home but could pay visits with a chaperone."[15] She had to be proficient at languages and music.

Which brings us to the eighteenth century and *Fanny Hill*, a novel which was banned, but offers great insights into the sexual practices of the day, including prostitution. One of its themes was that prostitution is seen as a possible road out of poverty. And there was *Moll Flanders*, who also used prostitution to climb out of servitude. Prostitution was widespread all through Europe during this period and there is much literature to illustrate this, from the above-mentioned novels, to novels by Joseph Fielding and in France the famous *Manon Lescault*.

In the nineteenth century prostitution develops even more, but there is backlash to sexuality in general. From the literature we know that prostitution was part of the mainstream, especially in France, as we see in such novels as Zola's *Nana*, and de Maupassant's *The Lady of the Camelias*, as well as in Manet's painting of *Nana*, and in the poetry of Baudelaire.

The backlash came from the medical profession who railed against masturbation and advised married women to have sex less than once a month. This is partly because of the myth of motherhood, which made it unseemly for women to have sex. So as Ringdal points out, especially in France, but probably all through parts of Europe, and elsewhere, "There are good reasons to believe that French men, married or unmarried, had a lot more sex with prostitutes than between their conjugal sheets."[16]

In England Josephine Butler started a moral crusade about women's place being in the home. In 1874 the World Organization for the Struggle Against State Regulation of Prostitution was founded, with Butler as secretary-general. In her first book, *A Letter to the Mothers of England*, she took on the issue of prostitution among Minors.

But this was challenged in many places. Napoleon Bonaparte argued that prostitution was necessary because otherwise military men would accost respectable women on the streets. And in 1881 the chief medical officer of Norway wrote that stopping prostitution would be like unplugging sewers.[17] Also at this time people were making connections between poverty and prostitution. By 1870 all of Europe, including the colonies, had adopted regulations based on a French model. This model included registration and medical check-ups.

According to Ringdal the years from 1870 through 1930 were the high time for prostitution all over the world. Thanks to steamships, women and girls could travel all over, and one found European women all over Asia, Africa and South America.[18]

The debate on prostitution continued through the century, and, of course, it is with us to this day. Some people argue for criminalization, some for legalization, others for decriminalization, others for charging clients. But until recently no one listened to the prostitutes themselves. It is to these voices we now turn.

In 1970 Margo St. James was falsely accused of prostitution, and as a result of seeing how badly the law worked, she formed COYOTE, Call Off Your Old Tired Ethics, which called for the decriminalization of prostitution. The feminist movement at the time embraced prostitutes but also felt that prostitution was largely due to poverty and the subjugation of women, so once economic conditions and liberation had been achieved, prostitution would disappear.[19]

The issue of prostitution was taken up by Kate Millett in her book, *The Prostitution Papers*. By this time feminists were not favorably disposed to prostitution, and saw it, along with pornography, as an evil. But prostitutes fought back using the pro-choice view that "it is my body and I can do with it what I want."

Prostitutes wanted to focus on the struggle against male violence and for self-determination. It is this latter issue that divided the pro and anti prostitution factions. The anti prostitution side saw prostitution as a form of exploiting women and saw prostitutes as weak and immature while Margo St James struck back with "A blow job is better than no job."[20]

The debate continues today but perhaps the best quote from a prostitute comes from a British call girl in 1980: "To say that a woman sells her body is bullshit. What she does is to give a customer access to her body for a short time, at a fixed price, just as a shrink allows a patient access to his brain for a higher price." And various sociologists who studied prostitution by actually talking to prostitutes found that the women had a positive view of their work.[21]

And now to hear actual prostitutes speak, I will quote from a book entitled *Red Light Labour: Sex Work, Regulation, Agency, and Resistance*. edited by Elya M. Durisin, Emily van der Meulen and Chris Bruckert. This book is a collection of pieces about the sex trades, including pieces by people in the trades. While the book is Canadian, it makes reference to other parts of the world as well. In the Preface, Valerie Scott, a sex worker and the president of a sex workers' union in Toronto points out that there are "at least 237 sex rights workers in over seventy countries worldwide." And she points out that "laws regulating sex work are important, not just in an obvious way for what they prohibit but also for the conditions they create and their influence on how sex workers are perceived."[22]

In the introductory chapter the editors point out that the "the ways in which sex work is conceptualized have a direct impact on how it is governed." The criminalization of sex work, for example sees both sex workers and the sex industry as public threats, and on the Swedish model where the clients and not the sex workers are arrested, sex workers are seen to be the victims of male exploitation.[23]

They go on to argue that a regulatory approach to the issue, as opposed to criminalization or complete decriminalization, which allows sex workers to access their rights, is supported by sex workers internationally, who define sex work "as a form of legitimate and socially valuable labor." This is the case since "Locating sex work as a form of labor not only challenges embedded stigmatic assumptions of deviance, immorality and pathology but also opens a rich analytical point of entry to think through these issues... In short, understanding sex work as a form of labor enables connections to be drawn between it and other forms of emotional, caring and/or service work..."[24]

Another point that needs to be made is that prostitution is not just a female trade. There are male prostitutes and female clients. As Ummni Kahn points out, "female clients exist but have been entirely overlooked by anti-prostitution advocates. The experiences of transgender, gender-non-binary, and gender-variant clients have also been ignored.

So let us look at this other side by exploring the work of a male prostitute.

River Redwood started as a prostitute at the age of 16. When riding a streetcar an older man who was sitting behind him told him it was his birthday and that he would pay to be beaten. Now a 47-year-old gay male porn performer, producer and director, River's biggest problem has been overcoming other people's misconceptions, stereotypes and prejudices regarding sex workers.[25]

He points out that male sex workers are everywhere, yet their existence is largely ignored. Few people, including the sex workers themselves, want to talk about it. He also makes the point that while many do it for fun or to make some extra money, some do it because they have no other options. But, when you come down to it, "being a male sex worker really isn't very different from any other kind of freelance job." The negative view of this is that because of his reputation is would be difficult to get a different kind of job. Through his experience as a sex worker he has "become acutely aware of the striking similarities between issues related to male and female sex work" regarding such things as stereotypes and that both are seen largely to be forced into doing what they are doing. He goes on to point out that no matter what other people do for a living, even if what they do has negative outcomes for others or for the environment, they still get more respect than sex workers.[26]

In talking about sex work in relation to other forms of work he argues that,

> We shouldn't be so quick to say that the porn industry is bad just because people are getting paid to perform sex. Pornography is hardly the only industry we should be focusing on when we talk about labor abuses and unfair work practices; as has been highly documented, harm and exploitation are abundant

in non-sex industry workplaces (Vosko, 2006; Workers Action Centre 2007). Although there is intense racism, classism, and ageism present in the sex industry, my feeling is that these "isms" and biases in male sex work reflect the power dynamics that exist in the larger society and within the capitalist economy itself.

And finally he argues that "No one is ever going to stop pornography or prostitution from taking place, nor should they try."[27]

In Canada there is an active sex worker rights movement. They had some success in the courts, but the next government brought in somewhat restrictive legislation which has not yet been challenged. Prostitution came under serious scrutiny in the 1970s when sex work was largely confined to neighborhoods with adult movie houses, strip clubs, adult bookstores, body rub parlors and other forms of adult entertainment. One way of dealing with this was to undertake redevelopment of these areas. The result was that sex workers moved to other neighborhoods. Sex workers were being harassed so they began to speak out. Groups such as COYOTE and BEAVER (Better End All Vicious Erotic Repression) were formed. Later this was changed to CASH (Coalition Against Street Harassment).

Things changed in the 80s with the HIV/AIDS epidemic when sex worker health became an issue and public health agencies adopted a harm reduction policy while sex workers were able to articulate their ability to institute safe sex practices.

Today various groups of sex workers are lobbying governments to change laws to allow for safety of sex workers.

METAPHYSICS

We see that there are important distinctions to be made between slavery, human trafficking, and prostitution. Slavery, and human trafficking, which is a form of slavery, is clearly immoral and illegal. Yet they persist mainly due to individual greed and a disregard for others.

Prostitution, or sex work, can be seen in a more positive light and needs to be properly understood and regulated, rather than criminalized.

EPISTEMOLOGY

We saw that slavery and prostitution have existed though most of human history but have been treated differently.

VALUES

Values play roles in at least three aspects of prostitution. First there are the values of the people who seek the services of sex workers. Second there are the values of the sex workers themselves. And third are the values of the various institutions and groups who oppose sex work.

If there were no demand for sex work, there would not be an issue. I have always found it interesting that on the one hand there is a demand for sex work in our, and in other, society(ies), while on the other hand there are factions in those same societies that thoroughly oppose sex work. And based on past experiences, we have seen that many people who oppose sex work have partaken of such work.

Part of the problem, I believe, is the conflicted views societies have regarding sexuality. In more puritanical societies, sexuality is frowned upon generally and is seen primarily as a form of reproduction and not of pleasure. And we saw above, when the medical profession saw women as fragile and sex only for childbearing, men were encouraged to seek out sex workers to satisfy their needs. Also, if we recall Freud's work, so many of his women clients who were suffering from some form of hysteria were exhibiting their symptoms due to repressed sexuality.

On the one hand, societies repress sexuality, but on the other hand those same societies realize the need for sexual expression. Another point that can be made here is society's attitude towards women. One argument regarding sex work is that because society as a whole devalues the role of women, sex work is a lucrative from of work available to them. This point gains some credibility when we learn that women, on the whole, earn significantly less than men do for the same work. But this point completely misses the role of male sex workers.

There is no escaping our sexuality. And as we have seen, societies over the millennia have treated sexuality differently. One of the lessons to be learned from this history is that we must acknowledge our sexuality and create social values that reflect this lesson. How this is to be done depends, of course, on the nature of the society in question.

This brings us back to the demand for sex work. As long as there is a demand for it, sex work will be with us. The reasons for the demand can be individual or social, or how individuals react to social constraints.

And this brings us to the sex workers themselves. As we have seen there are two distinct categories of sex work: those that involve coercion and those that do not. There is no moral justification for any kind of coercion. Coercion can also be seen as a form of human trafficking if, for whatever reason, people are forced into working in the sex trade.

But as we have also seen, people have made the choice to work in the sex trade, and many seem quite happy to do so. What they want is recognition of their choices, and proper protection from possibly violent clients. A form of legalization or decriminalization, with the right to organize and set up shop off the streets would be a good start.

Whether sex work is a desirable job choice is another question. It will probably never turn up in a list of college majors, or high school career choices. Sex workers will probably never be included in job fairs. But, if our attitudes towards sex work change, perhaps all of this can happen.

And finally, what are the values of the people who oppose sex work, who would like to see it abolished?

Some, of course, are religious or social conservatives who see sex work as a threat to family life. Yet, as we saw above, because of the negative view of women and sexuality, an argument for sex work was made to protect women. And some feminists opposed sex work on the grounds that it degraded women. Thus the thrust of the anti sex work movements stem from a view of protecting women, even if the sense of protection of one group would not be accepted by the other group.

LOGIC

In trying to make connections between how the issue is seen and how it affects people, here, as in so many other conflicting issues, there is little middle ground. But when actually looking at what is happening, it must be realized that the sex trade will not, at least in the near future, be abolished.

CONCLUSIONS

So where are we?

Serious behaviors such as slavery and trafficking are clearly immoral and unjustifiable. To treat people as commodities is wrong, yet, it still happens. Too many people put their own financial wellbeing ahead of any moral concerns for other people.

The sex trades provide a whole different set of concerns. On the one hand we see people opposed to the sex trades, for a variety of reasons. And we see many groups split on the issue. Feminists have primarily seen sex work as a form of exploitation of women, and often link it to porn. Back in the 70s the rallying cry was: porn is the theory; rape is the practice. But we have seen today this is not the case. And when looking at the porn industry the focus was always on the women but never the men. This was also the case for sex work in general. Yet men also work in both trades.

As long as there is a demand for sex work, it will most likely exist. Some people may get into it for quick money, while others seem to actually like the work. But for whatever reason people get into sex work we must accept the fact of its existence.

From a moral standpoint we must be concerned about the welfare of sex workers. There is a concept which I see as coming out of the medical oath of "Do No Harm" and that is a concept known as harm reduction. Even if we do not approve of a particular practice, we want to protect the people involved in that practice. For example, to curtail the spread of disease due to shared needles by drug users, needle exchanges and safe injection sites were set up. This also helped to prevent deaths from overdosing. In no way did these practices condone the use of drugs, but they were set up as forms of social safeguards, to protect both the drug users and society at large.

When applied to sex work, this approach would involve listening to the people in the practice to find out what they need for their protection. This might involve decriminalization or legalization, or legitimizing old-fashioned bawdy houses in order to get sex workers off the streets for their safety. And we must be concerned about the spread of sexually transmitted diseases from syphilis to HIV/AIDS. How these things can be accomplished will vary from community to community, but action must be taken.

The one topic that was not discussed here is why is there such a demand for sex work. Having an answer to that might go a long way to solving what are perceived as the moral and social problems coming from the existence of the sex trades.

NOTES

1. Ringdal, Nils Johan, *Love For Sale*: *A World History of Prostitution*, Translated by Richard Daly, (New York: Grove Press, 2004) 4.
2. Ringdal, 6.
3. Ringdal, 12.
4. Ringdal 16.
5. Ringdal 17–18.
6. *Special Action Programme to Combat Forced Labour* (20 May 2014). "Profits and poverty: The economics of forced labour"(PDF). International Labour Organization. p.4.
7. Ringdal, 54.
8. Ringdal, 69–70.
9. Ringdal, 86.
10. Ringdal, 95.

11. Ringdal, 110.
12. Ringdal, 115.
13. Ringdal, 137.
14. Ringdal, 175–179
15. Ringdal, 183.
16. Ringdal, 148–149.
17. Ringdal, 260–261.
18. Ringdal, 313.
19. Ringdal, 369–371.
20. Ringdal, 366–367.
21. Ringdal, 381.
22. Durisin, Elya M, Emily van der Meulen, Chris Bruckert. *Red Light Labour*: *Sex Work, Regulation, Agency and Resistance*. (Vancouver: UBC Press, 2018), xii.
23. Durisin et al., 5–6.
24. Durisin et al., 9–10.
25. Durisin et al., 167.
26. Durisin et al., 168–171.
27. Durisin et al., 172.

Chapter Six

The Environment

METAPHYSICS

A discussion of the environment is multi-faceted. In a basic sense, the environment is a general topic where we have concerns about the world in which we live. This involves how we farm, what we eat, how we dispose of waste, what pollution does to the environment and, of course, global warming or climate change.

In Western society a good place to begin our discussion is with the story of creation. In Genesis 1 we are told,

> And God said: Let the earth bring forth the living creature after its kind, cattle, and creeping thing, and beast of the earth after its kind. And it was so. And God made the beast of the earth after its kind, and the cattle after their kind, and everything that creepeth on the ground after its kind; and God saw it was good. And God said, let us make man in our image, after our likeness; and let them have dominion over the fish of the sea, and over the fowl of the air, and over the cattle, and over all the earth.

The issue is about the word "dominion." In one sense it means "dominion over" which implies taking care of or looking after creation. We have a responsibility to nature. In another sense it means domination, where mankind can do what he wants to nature. This is the basis for disagreements about the environment to this day. Indeed, the very argument over climate change can, at least in part, be traced to this distinction. Either we look after nature or we exploit it.

When we apply dominion we get two opposing views regarding our relationship to nature. On the one side we get the view which involves our control over nature where nature exists for us. On this view humans see themselves as separate from nature, hence their dominion over nature. Nature exists to serve humans. On the other side where dominion is understood as looking after nature, humans see themselves as part of nature and, therefore, nature must be cared for. Also involved here is how to think about nature for the future. Will nature always be there regardless of how we treat it or are there limits to nature implying the need for conservation?

The main issues facing humankind today include human overpopulation, exploitation of nature, land degradation including factory farming, industrialization and its effects including greenhouse gas production, the use of dams and the use of carbon based fuels, resource depletion and its effects on the land, and a host of related issues.

EPISTEMOLOGY

One way to look at the issue is historically. The questions of environmental history date back to antiquity.

The Origins and Institutionalization of Environmental History (as a Self-conscious Enterprise)

Like every twist and turn within intellectual life, environmental history has countless and tangled roots. Some of the earliest extant texts, such as the Epic of Gilgamesh, deal with environmental change generated by human action (cutting cedar forests in this case). Many scholars of long ago, notably Ibn Khaldun and Montesquieu, found in the variations in the natural world, climate especially, a key to human behavior. Historical geographers since the 1870s charted landscape change, especially in Europe. For professional historians, awareness of geographical constraints and influences has long been a hallmark, although not a universal. Fernand Braudel, in what was probably the twentieth century's most influential book among professional historians, devoted a large chunk of La Méditerranée to geography and environment.

But environmental history as a self-conscious undertaking dates only to about 1970 and, like so much in intellectual life, drew its energy from society at large. Around the world, of course, the 1960s and 1970s witnessed the coalescence of popular environmentalism as a cultural and political force. It was stronger in some place than in others, and took different shapes in different contexts. In the United States it helped a few historians, initially almost all of whom were scholars of U.S. history, to come together both intellectually and institutionally to launch environmental history as a self-conscious undertaking. Among them were Roderick Nash, John Opie, Donald Worster, Susan Flader, and a historian of the ancient Mediterranean, Donald Hughes. By some accounts Nash, author of Wilderness and the American Mind, an intellectual history of an environmental subject, was the first to employ the term "environmental history."

Perhaps the one book that really brought the issue to light was Rachel Carson's *Silent Spring*, published in 1962, which highlighted how the indiscriminate use of pesticides caused human illnesses as well as destroying aspects of nature. This book eventually led to the banning of DDT and other pesticides once people saw the actual harm they were doing to both themselves and the environment at large. Thus it was knowledge of the effects of the chemicals which led to its ban. These pesticides were not just killing the pests they were intended o kill but were also killing non pests and were having an effect up the food chain leading to human illnesses.

In looking at various environmental issues we will also be looking at the scientific data that has been compiled on the issues. This will range from big data regarding global warming to more specific data regarding more specific issues.

VALUES

Here we will look at values in two ways. One way is how people's values influence their views on the issues. In a way, this relates to the two views of "dominion." The second way is to look at values in terms of results or consequences of our actions with regard to nature, or the environment. And, where the consequences are bad, we will also look at motives for maintaining bad environmental practices.

Discussion

A good way to start is to list some of the recent disasters that have led to our concerns. We can go back to the dust bowl days of the 1930s, where drought caused the soil to turn to dust and Oklahoman soil was windblown all the way to Washington D.C. In the 1960s Cleveland's Cuyahoga River caught fire because of pollutants in the water. There were the London smog crisis of 1952 which left four thousand people dead, various oil spills such as the Exxon Valdez, which damaged wildlife, Three Mile Island, the Chernobyl and Fukushima nuclear plant problems causing radioactive leaking and damaging natural environments as well as human health. And, of course, there is the negative effect that fluorocarbons have had on the ozone layer.

The point of this brief list is that, with the exception of the dust bowl drought, all were events brought about by human action.

But first let us define what we are talking about. Global warming is the long-term rise in the average temperature over the planet. It been demonstrated by direct temperature measurements around the globe and by measurements of various local phenomena. The term refers to changes made by human caused effects to global temperatures by such things as increased greenhouse gases, fewer trees and polluted waterways.

Some deniers of the human aspect of climate change point to the fact that historically we have seen great climate changes in prehistoric times, such as the great ice age, but climate measurements today have shown that the increase in temperatures in this century have been greater than at any other time and these changes in temperature can be directly related to human conduct. The Intergovernmental Panel on Climate Change Fifth Assessment concluded: "It is extremely likely that human influence has been the dominant cause of the observed warming since the mid-20th century."[1]

The effects of global warming include rising seas, changes in precipitation patterns and more violent weather patterns. Rising seas are mainly caused by melting ice from glaciers and permafrost, and could lead to the destruction of coastlines affecting millions of people. Changing weather patterns are a threat to crop yields and ultimately to our food security.

All the evidence points to the fact that global warming is real and that human activity is a cause. Before going into what we can do about it let us look at the evidence and at why people deny that human activity is a cause of the cause of global warming. Many of these so-called climate change deniers do not deny the climate is changing. They just deny that human activity is a main source of the change.

The main piece of information that leads to the conclusion that human activity is a main cause of the current warming can be seen from data compiled by NASA. For the first time in all of history the amount of carbon dioxide in the atmosphere has exceeded three hundred parts per million. The highest ever recorded was at that number over 300,000 years ago. Today it has exceeded four hundred parts per million.

The NASA site points out that the heat trapping nature of carbon dioxide was known by the middle of the nineteenth century. Today we have all kinds of knowledge to show that the rapid increase in warming is due to human activity. "Ice cores from Greenland, Antarctica and tropical mountain glaciers shows that the earth's climate responds to changes in greenhouse gas levels. Ancient evidence can also be found in tree rings, ocean sediments, coral reefs, and layers of sedimentary rocks. This ancient, or paleoclimate, evidence reveals that current warming is occurring roughly ten times faster than the average rate of ice-age recovery."[2]

The site goes on to point out that,

> The planet's average surface temperature has risen about 1.62 degree Fahrenheit (0.9 degrees Celsius) since the late nineteenth century, a change driven largely by increased carbon dioxide and other human-made emissions into the atmosphere. Most of the warming occurred in the past 35 years with the five warmest years on record taking place since 2010. Not only was 2016 the warmest year on record, but eight of the twelve months that make up the year—from January through September, with the exception of June—were the warmest on record for those respective months.[3]

The site also points out that oceans are warming, that ice sheets in Greenland and the Arctic are shrinking and that sea levels are rising.

In the section on causes, the site explains the greenhouse effect, a process in which certain gases in the atmosphere prevent heat from escaping. Long-lived gases that remain in the atmosphere and do not change with temperature changes are described as "forcing" climate change. Gases that contribute to the greenhouse effect include water vapor, nitrous oxide, carbon dioxide and methane.

> Water vapor is the most abundant greenhouse gas which acts as a feedback to the climate. Water vapor increases as the atmosphere warms, but so does the possibility of clouds and precipitation, making these some of the most important feedback mechanisms to the greenhouse effect.
>
> Carbon dioxide is a minor but important component of the atmosphere. It is released through natural processes such as respiration and volcano eruptions and through human activities such as deforestation, land use changes, and burning fossil fuels. Humans have increased the atmospheric carbon dioxide concentration by more than a third since the Industrial revolution began. This is the most important long-lived "forcing" of climate change.
>
> Methane. A hydrocarbon gas produced both through natural sources and human activities, including the decomposition of wastes in landfills, agriculture, and especially rice cultivation, as well as ruminant digestion and manure management associated with domestic livestock. On a molecule-for-molecule basis, methane is a far more active greenhouse gas than carbon dioxide, but also one which is much less abundant in the atmosphere.
>
> Nitrous oxide. A powerful greenhouse gas produced by soil cultivation practices, especially the use of commercial and organic fertilizers, fossil fuel combustion, nitric acid production, and biomass burning.
>
> Chlorofluorocarbons (CFCs). Synthetic compounds entirely of industrial origin used in a number of applications, but now largely regulated in production and release to the atmosphere by international agreement for their ability to contribute to destruction of the ozone layer. They are also greenhouse gases.[4]

The Role of Human Activity

In its Fifth Assessment Report, the Intergovernmental Panel on Climate Change, a group of 1,300 independent scientific experts from countries all over the world under the auspices of the United Nations, concluded that there is a more than 95 percent probability that human activities over the past 50 years have warmed our planet.

The industrial activities that our modern civilization depends upon have raised atmospheric carbon dioxide levels from 280 parts per million to four hundred parts per million in the last 150 years. The panel also concluded that there is a better than 95 percent probability that human-produced greenhouse gases such as carbon dioxide, methane and nitrous oxide have caused much of the observed increase in Earth's temperatures over the past fifty years.

The panel's full Summary for Policymakers report is online.[5]

And finally, the NASA site states that,

> Multiple studies published in peer-reviewed scientific journals show that 97 percent or more of actively publishing climate scientists agree: Climate-warming trends over the past century are extremely likely due to human activities. In addition, most of the leading scientific organizations worldwide have issued public statements endorsing this position.

So the facts are in. The current change in climate, or global warming, while having some natural factors, is largely caused by human activity.

Climate change denial simply denies the scientific data. So, in the light of all the evidence, why would people deny that human activity is causing this change? One aspect of this denial isn't really denial but people's reluctance or inability to come to terms with these changes as it relates to their own lives. For example, while they can acknowledge that climate change is due to human activity, they cannot see how it impacts on their behavior. They see no need to give up their big SUVs or stop taking planes for travel or stop using plastics, and so on.

But perhaps the largest group of deniers are people who have industrial interests which would be affected by having to change how they do business, people with specific political and ideological interests which would be interfered with by acknowledging that climate change is caused by human activity. The book *Climate Change Denial: Heads in the Sand*, documents all forms of climate change denial with data from numerous sources. From its website:

> The politics of global warming have been affected by climate change denial and the political global warming controversy, undermining the efforts to act on climate change or adapting to the warming climate. Those promoting denial

commonly use rhetorical tactics to give the appearance of a scientific controversy where there is none.

And it goes on to say that,

Organised campaigning to undermine public trust in climate science is associated with conservative economic policies and backed by industrial interests opposed to the regulation of CO2 emissions.[20] Climate change denial has been associated with the fossil fuels lobby, the Koch brothers, industry advocates and conservative think tanks, often in the United States. More than ninety percent of papers sceptical on climate change originate from right-wing think tanks.

Since the late 1970s, oil companies have published research broadly in line with the standard views on global warming. Despite this, oil companies organized a climate change denial campaign to disseminate public disinformation for several decades, a strategy that has been compared to the organized denial of the hazards of tobacco smoking by the tobacco industry.

Thus those who deny climate change, or that human activity has anything to do with climate change, are people whose businesses and beliefs would be directly affected by such an acknowledgement. Indeed, if a fossil fuel company executive were to accept that burning fossil fuels is a cause of climate change, they would either have to quit their job or start trying to change how the company operates, possibly by shifting from extracting oil or gas from the ground to building solar panels or wind turbines. And, of course, people with a lot invested in their jobs or companies, or even ways of life or ways in which they see the world, do not want those things to change. So instead of accepting the facts of global warming, they either deny it outright, or say the science is bad, because they are not prepared to make major changes to their lives.

So in a real sense what we have here is a clash of values. As in the abortion debate where the two sides start from totally different places, we have a new set of facts which lead to a re-evaluation of our values, since these facts have a direct impact on how we live. If I am not prepared to make any significant changes in how I live or how I think about the world, I will not accept these new facts.

In the rest of this chapter I want to look at some specific aspects of life where global warming is having an effect, and to look at the specific controversies in those issues. I am going to limit the discussion to two issues: energy and food production, especially since there is an overlap with regard to the issue of biofuels.

To begin, I want to quote Thomas Easton from the introduction to the chapter on energy from his anthology *Taking Sides*: *Clashing Views on Environmental Issues*.

Humans cannot live and society cannot exist without producing environmental impacts. The reason is very simple: Humans cannot live and society cannot exist without using resources (e.g., oil, water ore, wood, space, plants, animals, oil, sunlight) and these resources come from the environment. Many of these resources (e.g., wood, oil, coal, water, wind, sunlight, uranium) have to do with energy. The environmental impacts come from what must be done to obtain these resources and what must be done to dispose of the wastes generated in the process of obtaining and using them. The issues that arise are whether and how we should deal with the wastes, and whether alternative answers to these questions may be preferable to the answers that experts think they already have.[6]

We already know that we must severely lessen our dependence on fossil fuels. Fossil fuels not only cause smog and greenhouse gases when burned, but their production and transportation cause other problems, such as oil spills, which have a negative effect on the environment. But can we get off the use of fossil fuels quickly? The answer is probably no, since so much of our lives depends on these fuels. It would probably be fairly easy to retrofit homes from using gas or oil to solar and/or wind power. But that would still take an enormous amount of labor, person power and money, so it cannot be done overnight.

And we still drive our cars. While more and more people are buying all electric or hybrid cars, it will still take years to get people to change, if for no other reason than financial ones, even if financial incentives from governments are available. But even with electric cars, energy still has to be produced to charge the batteries. Other forms of incentives to get rid of fossil fuels could be the use of a carbon tax, which many economists say is effective, and to stop subsidies to fossil fuel producing companies.

Another source of energy to look at is nuclear energy, which is clean, but there are two problems with it: one is the cost of building nuclear plants, and the second is the disposal of the nuclear waste.

So while the long-term goal would be to replace fossil fuels, some realistic time frames would have to be set. Clearly there are solutions, but to implement them will take time, money and the will to change.

And on to agriculture.

An agricultural issue which directly relates to environmental concerns is that of biofuels. Is producing corn for biofuels, which would replace some amount of fossil fuel used for cars, environmentally beneficial? While there is some biofuel production going on now, the question becomes whether it should become more widespread.

On the positive side the use of biofuels can reduce the amount of fossil fuels we burn. If we are careful and do not encroach too much on food growing land but use other, less fertile land, the use of biofuels can make an impact on the production of greenhouse gases. This would be even better if various forms of bio waste were used.

On the negative side, the main concern is the use of food land to produce biofuel, thereby reducing the amount of food and raising the price of agricultural products. Another consideration is that the energy used to produce biofuels, from harvesting to processing, can actually use more energy that it produces.

This brings up the issue regarding our food supply. We hear about starvation around the world. Some of these situations are caused by bad politics and others by changes in weather leading to changes in harvests. But the overriding question is whether we can we produce enough food to feed the world's population.

We have heard about the population problem for centuries. The most famous statement comes from nineteenth century economist Thomas Malthus who argued that population grew geometrically while food supply grew arithmetically. Thus population would soon out pass food production. In different terms, this is also a concern of Marvin Harris who always saw problems of growth associated with problems of societal fall.

The overpopulation issue has been stated and stated and is still with us. But the other side of the issue has been gaining in discussion. As Sean Lanahan argues "The earth is more than able to support not only seven billion souls, but up to two to four times as much with a little work and a little impact on other life."[7]Using statistics from the Food and Agriculture Organization of the United Nations, he shows that the earth currently produces enough food to feed double our current population, and that there is enough land for all this production. If we need more food we can use additional growing resources such as seawater greenhouses.

Then there is the distribution problem:[8]

> Consumers have difficulty purchasing food because of their inability to access markets and/or their inability to afford the costs. On the other end, farmers cannot sell their produce for the similar reasons. Therefore, the main problems with the current distribution system are the lack of markets, the inadequacy of transportation to markets, and the inability to afford the costs of production and consumption.

And then there is political interference, with corruption and wars limiting people's access to food.

Finally we should mention organic farming. Like everything else it has its pro and cons. On the positive side farming without the use of fertilizers and pesticides is good for the environment in that contaminants are not added to the soil which eventually run off either into our groundwater or into our rivers and streams and eventually into our drinking water. On the negative side organic farming produces less, which increases the costs. Another factor is that people, at least in North America, want their produce to look perfect. And because pesticides are not used, some organically grown crops do not look perfect, which leads to wastage.

All this being said, our ability to produce food is still finite, therefore we must ultimately be concerned about population growth. And, as population grows demand to cut down rainforests to produce will lead to more environmental degradation. Thus, ultimately, population growth is a factor to be concerned about.

CONCLUSIONS

Metaphysics

As we have seen the issues around climate change or global warming are real. The climate is changing. The dispute is between people who say that human activity is a cause of the change and people who say that it is just a normal process.

Epistemology

We have seen data from NASA and other sources which prove that human activity is at least a primary, if not the sole, cause of the current change in climate. There is no disputing the data. We could argue whether human activity is the sole cause of climate change or one of the causes, but human activity is clearly a factor.

Values

The values of the people who deny that human activity is a cause of climate change appear to be motivated by personal concerns. They see acting to curtail human activity as impinging on their activities. And in so doing they put their personal concerns above more general concerns about their fellow humans, and the environment.

People who value their fellow people and the environment will act to change how human activity affects the climate. This can be done in a number of ways. We can change our personal habits by using less of the things that add to the problem and we can prod our politicians and industrialists to act on the issue.

Two areas where we can quickly change our behaviors are our use of fossil fuels and plastic. We can drive less, we can buy hybrid or electric cars, we can use mass transit more. And we can stop buying water in plastic bottles. But, of course, the major factor is industrial pollution and this can only be lowered by the use of serious political will on the parts of governments. Changing how we use energy, or changing our forms of energy, will lead to displacements of people working in the fossil fuel and related industries. But as new jobs develop in alternative fuel industries, these workers can transition. Governments at all levels will have to be involved.

Logic

Logic shows that by following the facts we cannot deny that human activity is a cause, and most likely the primary cause of the current situation. Thus logic compels us to act. But how to act is a difficult question, for there are no perfect solutions. As we have seen, all human activity has an environmental impact, so choices have to be made which involves the lesser impacts. And we also have to consider available resources, which can limit our choices. But, to solve the problem, choices must be made and behaviours must change.

NOTES

1. IPCC AR5 WG1 Summary for Policymakers 2013, p.17.
2. "Climate Change: How do we Know?" Global Climate Change, NASA, https://www.climate.nasa.gov/evidence/. Site checked July 31, 2020.
3. "NASA, NOAA Data Show 2016 Warmest Year on Record Globally," NASA News and Feature Releases, Goddard Institute for Space Studies, NASA, January 18, 2017, http://www.giss.nasa.gov/research/news/20170118/. Site checked July 31.2020.
4. "The Causes of Climate Change," Global Climate Change, NASA, https://www.climate.nasa.gov/causes/ Site checked July 31, 2020.
5. "Summary for Policymakers," Intergovernmental Panel on Climate Change, United Nations, February 2019 www.ipcc.ch/site/assets/uploads/sites/2/2019/05/SR15_SPM_version_report_LR.pdf. Site checked July 31.2020.
6. Easton, Thomas, Durisin, Elya M, Emily van der Meulen, Chris Bruckert. *Red Light Labour: Sex Work, Regulation, Agency and Resistance*. (Vancouver: UBC Press, 2018) 106.
7. Sean Lanahan, in Easton, 196.
8. "Inadequate Food Distribution Systems," Mission 2014: Feeding the World, 2014, http://12.000.scripts.mit.edu/mission2014/problems/inadequate-food-distribution-systems. Site checked July 31.2020.

Chapter Seven

Guns

METAPHYSICS

We could ask why guns exist. What are they for? Why do we need them? But while these questions have merit on an abstract level, our concern here is to come up with an understanding of the reality of gun use.

Guns can be used for a number of things. The most obvious is as weapons of war. They are used for hunting, and for self-defence, and for recreation. Guns are also used in the commission of crimes.

Most countries have various forms of legislation dealing with the acquisition and use of guns. Recently, due to various actions, other countries have amended their legislation. But the big controversy exists primarily in The United States and to a lesser degree in Canada.

The controversy in the United States centers around the second amendment to the Constitution, which states,

> A well-regulated Militia, being necessary to the security of a free State, the right of the people to keep and bear Arms, shall not be infringed.

The controversy centers around the limits of the right to bear arms. Some people just look at that phrase, while others look at the whole sentence. Do Americans have the right to bear arms under any and all conditions, or only to be able to serve in a militia to defend the country?

The debate, as it exists today, dates to the passage of the National Firearms Act of 1934, which was passed after prohibition era gangsterism peaked.

To be more specific, the issue, especially in the United States, has to do with the kinds of restrictions that can be placed on the right to bear arms. Can certain kinds of weapons be completely banned? Can restrictions be placed on who can purchase weapons? Can restrictions be placed on where and how weapons are bought and sold?

EPISTEMOLOGY

Here we will look at the policies of a few other countries, and a little history of the American situation.

In China, "According to PRC law, there are firearms regulations and according to those regulations 'whoever, in violation of firearm-control regulations, secretly keeps firearms or ammunition and refuses to relinquish them shall be sentenced to fixed-term imprisonment of not more than two years.'"[1]

Private ownership of firearms was first banned by the Qing dynasty which lasted from 1644 to 1911, though there are exceptions, such as in the time of war, or of political uprising.

In Finland citizens need permission to possess a firearm, which is given by the police and requires a valid reason. Permission can be denied if the applicant has a criminal background, has problems with alcohol and/or drugs, or has mental health problems. The right to possess a firearm in Finland does not include the right to carry it in public, except while hunting. At home, firearms must be kept under lock and key.

In Switzerland there is compulsory military service, where everyone is issued a proper weapon because, even after their service, all Swiss who served are considered reservists. All weapons must be kept under lock and key, and away from ammunition. Switzerland has one of the highest gun ownership rates in the world, along with one of the lowest crime rates.

In England there is no general talk of rights, since much of the constitution is by tradition. "Modern law exists only to curtail certain actions which are deemed illegal for the common good. There is English Common Law right to keep and bear arms for self protection but the ownership of certain arms is controlled for the common good."

According to the text of *Gun Ownership*: *The Right to Bear Arms and the Surrounding Controversy*, with regard to the American situation, "the right to bear arms is often presented in the context of military service and the broader right of self defense." The big debate is whether the right pertains to individuals or to the people acting collectively.[2]

Some court decisions favour individuals while other court decisions favor "the people" or the right of the state. 7 And of course the right to bear arms comes with military service.

The text goes on to point out that there are three models for discussing the second amendment. The first two models focus on the preamble or "purpose" clause, dealing with maintaining a well-regulated militia, while the third model focuses on the individual right to bear arms.

The first model holds that the people, collectively, have the right to bear arms, since the only reason to bear arms is to maintain a militia. The second model is similar to the first in that it holds that the right to bear arms exists for individuals actively serving in a militia, and that there may be regulations. The third model holds that individuals have a right to bear arms as much as the First Amendment protects the right of individuals to engage in free speech.

The main issue discussed in the context of the right to bear arms is that of self-defence. As the text points out, early theories made no distinction between defence of the person or defence of property. John Locke states in the Two Treatises on Government,

> ... the enjoyment of the property he has in this state is very unsafe, very unsecure. This makes him willing to quit a condition, which however free, is full of fears and continual dangers; and it is not without reason, that he seeks out, and is willing to join in a society with others, who are already united, or have a mind to unite, for the mutual preservation of their lives, liberties, and estates, which I call by the general name, property.[3]

For modern theories, the question of self-defence is one of moral authority within the nation which can set limits to obedience to the state and to individuals. This leads to different nations having different laws regarding what counts as self-defence and how the government or the individual can define any given situation. One result of this is that resolutions of debates on the issue all too often end up in the courts. And there are many court decisions on the issue.

With this background we turn to interpretations of the second amendment. In order to properly understand the amendment we must go back to English law to see where it all came from.

In England the right to bear arms is believed to have been established as a natural right. In American court decisions (District of Columbia v. Heller, 2008) this was seen as an individual right, having nothing to do with serving in a militia.

Both the British and the American bills of rights have to do with protecting the right to bear arms. In United States law until 2000, "it was believed to have been about solely preventing infringement by the federal government, while in the English case it protects Protestants from encroachment by the king."[4]

The case Heller and McDonald v Chicago (2010) ruled that the drafters of the second and fourteenth amendments intended handguns as being lawful for self-defence. The historical link between the English Bill of Rights and the second amendment has been acknowledged by the United States Supreme Court. This has led to discussions about what "bear arms" meant, largely in terms belonging to a militia or for personal use.

In recent years the powerful National Rifle Association has influenced the debate on whether there should be limitations on the right to bear arms. The NRA was founded back in 1871 as an organization dedicated to protect the second amendment and promote firearm ownership rights. The NRA sponsors firearm safety training as well as marksmanship events. Its main political activity is in lobbying members of congress on the principle that gun ownership is a civil liberty protected by the second amendment. Indeed, members of congress have ranked the NRA as the most powerful lobby organization in the country.[5]

The NRA has not only lobbied in favour of gun ownership based on the second amendment but has also intervened in cases involving gun ownership. They opposed the Brady Bill in 1993 which imposed an interim five-day waiting period for the purchase of a handgun, so that federally licensed dealers would be able to conduct background checks through the National Instant Criminal System on all potential buyers.

And, of course, the NRA has been criticized from all sides for its extreme positions. One of the issues is the availability of assault weapons to the general public. Many groups have opposed this but the NRA supports it.

VALUES

Values play a number of roles here. In one sense, each group—each viewpoint—on the issue of whether or not there should be some kind of limitation on what kinds of weapons can be bought, and whether there should be proper background checks on weapons buyers, all represent different values. They see the roles of guns differently. People who want to own guns see it as their right. People who want to limit gun ownership appear to be more concerned with the consequences of having lots of guns available to most people.

The intent of people who want to own guns is straightforward. Not only is it their perceived right, but many gun owners are also concerned about improper use of guns. Guns can be used to kill people, but can also be used for recreation. For example, in Switzerland, where almost all adults own guns, there is a huge use of gun ranges, but virtually no gun crimes. Since guns exist, and since many people end up in military service, why not just accept the fact that people have guns and must learn to use them responsibly?

This leads us to look at the consequences of gun ownership. According to data compiled by the CDC in 2017, 39,773 people died from gun related injuries in the United States. This includes murders, suicides, unintentional shootings, and law enforcement shootings. According to the same source, almost sixty percent of these deaths were suicides, while 37 percent (14,542) were murders.

The gun death rate in the United States is much higher than most other countries. In 2016, the most recent year for this study, the U.S. gun death rate was 10.6 per 100,000 people. In Canada the rate was 2.1 per 100,000 people, while in France, the rate was 2.7, Australia 1.0 and Germany 0.9, all per 100,000 people. But in other countries the rates are higher: El Salvador was 39.2, Venezuela 38.7, Guatemala 32.3 and Columbia 25.9, all per 100,000 people.

But the real issue is that of mass shootings. In 2018, 373 people died in mass shootings. And there are real concerns about all the mass shootings that have taken place in 2019. In 2017 handguns were involved in 64 percent of all murders while so-called assault weapons were involved in four percent.[6] Thus the consequences of gun ownership can be fatal.

LOGIC

Here we have to make connections between our values and the information we have. Do we want to spare lives? Do we want people to have access to guns? And if so, do we want background checks to try to ensure the guns will not be misused? And do we want to limit the kinds of guns available to people?

DISCUSSION

Since the big issue around what to do about guns is American, let us start with how the issue is seen there. We do this by looking at the two main interpretations of the Second Amendment. One focuses on the idea of the standing militia and the other on the right to bear arms.

The belief about the militia is complex, especially since the United States has a standing army. There is no need for militias as envisioned in the eighteenth century. Thus, to take this argument to its conclusion, since there is no need for militias, there is no need to bear arms.

This argument, while logically valid, is a bit simplistic since it avoids dealing with the realities of gun ownership today. But it still has some force regarding the kinds of weapons that might be available. For example, if there is no militia, there need not be any weapons available that could be considered militia or military styled. So no assault rifles should be made available to the public.

Of course, if one has served in the military, the question arises as to whether weapons should be kept or returned to the military. As we saw in Switzerland, since everyone who serves is still considered a member of the reserves, they are required to keep their weapons, but under strict laws governing their storage and use.

But this does not address the question of other forms of guns, such as pistols and hunting rifles. We could ask why such things even exist. But, again, that is to avoid the realities of their existence and use.

Hunting is an acceptable form of behaviour. Animals are used for food, and their hides are used for clothing. We eat animals whether they are hunted or farmed. So rifles for hunting can be justified.

Pistols are used largely for self-defence. They are used by law enforcement. But as we have seen pistols are the number one cause of gun deaths, and the number one instrument of suicides. So, can a case be made for the restriction of sales of pistols?

This question arises out of the fact that there are no militias. In this sense, one cannot justify the ownership of most weapons. But people do own these weapons. Thus, even though the absence of militias makes a strong case for the controlling or even banning of many weapons, the issue is not seen as relevant.

Which brings us to the second interpretation of the Second Amendment which focuses just on the right to bear arms, ignoring the main reason for that right. Given the wording of the Second Amendment, the role of the militia is still relevant. But since there is no militia, and people do own guns, we have to look at the reality of the situation.

Americans seem to love their guns. We can say that they live in a gun culture. Whether this has to do with the old frontier mentality, good marketing by gun companies, influence from the National Rifle Association, or some combination of all three, Americans still seem to love their guns. So we have to deal with the reality of the situation. In one sense the question becomes what can be done to make society safer. When compared to other countries, Americans own about 120 guns per one hundred people, while in Canada the number is around 35 guns per hundred people. In Norway it is about 25 per one hundred and in England it is less than ten per hundred.

With regard to homicides, in the United States in 2016 there were approximately 110 deaths per 100,000 people, while in Canada the number is less than ten. It is even lower in Norway and England.

Most people favour some kind of background checks. According to a 2016 survey, 86 percent of registered voters supported background checks. For Republicans the number was 79% and for Democrats the number was 88 percent. These checks exist when dealing with registered gun owners but do not exist when buying at gun shows or from other gun owners. This is where the gap needs to be filled.

So laws can be passed for background checks to cover all aspects of gun buying. The next question is what kinds of guns should be on the market. Clearly, since there is no militia, military style weapons have no place in the civilian market. Rifles for hunting are acceptable, but buyers should have to pass some kind of check to prove they are hunters.

The real concern is about handguns since they are prolific and since they are most used in gun deaths. In Canada handguns are restricted weapons. This limits how many can be bought, and by whom.

CONCLUSIONS

Metaphysics

As we have seen the main issues regarding the use of guns are who can buy them and what kinds of guns can be bought.

Epistemology

Here we looked at how guns are used and the justification for having guns, as well as the death and destruction caused by guns.

Values

Here we saw that different kinds of values play a role in gun ownership. One is cultural, but we can also look at intentions and consequences.

People buy guns for different reasons. The main reasons appear to be for hunting and for self protection.

But let us look at consequences. Since handguns seem to be the largest factor in gun deaths, maybe the reasons people give for buying these guns is not the real case. But whatever the reason, one way to stop gun deaths, a consequence of owning guns, is to limit the number of guns.

Logic

By looking at all these factors logic leads us to the conclusions that we need background checks on gun buyers, not just at regular dealers but also at gun shows and online. In order to prevent gun deaths, the guns that figure prominently in those deaths should also be limited. We have already provided good reasons for banning military type weapons for sale to the public, but perhaps, if not banning hand guns outright, we might make it more difficult to purchase them.

NOTES

1. McHale, Kolby, ed. *Gun Ownership: The Right to Bear Arms and the Surrounding Controversy*, no publication data, all articles taken from the internet 1.
2. McHale, 6.
3. John Locke, quoted by McHale, 17.
4. McHale, 26.
5. Mchale, 226.
6. "What the Data Says About Gun Deaths in the U.S." Fact Tank, Pew Research, August 16, 2019, https://www.pewresearch.org/fact-tank/2019,08/16/what-the-data-says about-gun-deaths-in-the-u-s/ Site checked July 31, 2020.

Chapter Eight

Drugs

METAPHYSICS

Drugs of one kind or another have been used by societies all over the world and through all historical periods. But since the nineteenth century some societies have made some drugs illegal. This has led to various social issues. Also, especially in recent years, there has been a great deal of abuse with of prescription drugs. Various solutions have been proposed. One is to see all dealings with illegal drugs, and abuse of legal drugs, as a criminal issue. Others see it as a health issue, and others just see it in terms of trying to reduce the harm done by such drug use.

So do we keep all aspects of this kind of drug use in the criminal code and jail people who both sell and use these drugs? Or do we take drugs out of the criminal code and treat drug use as a health issue, while perhaps still keeping the illegal sale of these drugs in the criminal code? Do we soften this by setting up safe sites for drug use to prevent either the spread of disease through shared needles, or accidental overdoses? Or do we legalize but maintain controls on the drugs, keeping drug use as a health issue, but taking the sale of drugs out of private or criminal hands, and have government stores or doctors, or licensed facilities, issue drugs?

EPISTEMOLOGY

Different societies have prohibited different drugs. For example, in the Unites States opioids and similar drugs, including marijuana, are illegal but alcohol is perfectly legal, though, to some extent, restricted by age and by being heavily taxed. In strict Muslim countries alcohol is banned, yet other drugs are legal. The Church of Jesus Christ of Latter-Day Saints bans the use of coffee.

The Muslim ban on alcohol, attributed to passages in the Qur'an, dates from the seventh century. This ban included anything that could be considered an intoxicant, so also included hashish. In the Ottoman Empire Murad IV attempted to ban coffee as it was seen as an intoxicant, but this was overturned after his death in 1640.

In more recent times the first law passed regulating drugs was the Pharmacy Act 1868 in the United Kingdom. The act set controls on the distribution of poisons and drugs, including opium. This did lead to a significant decrease in deaths due to opium overuse. In the United States the drug law was passed in 1875 banning the smoking of opium in Chinese opium dens. Other similar laws were passed in the United States. Chinese people tended to smoke opium while white people used laudanum, which was a tincture of opium. Thus it mattered both who you were and how you used the drug.

The next major banning of drugs was Prohibition in the United States. Alcohol was the most common drug in the United States and there was great pressure to ban it. This also happened in Finland. The ban was lifted in Finland in 1932 and in the United States in 1933. The implications of prohibition are interesting in that the demand for alcohol continued, leading to all kinds of illegal activity. When something is illegal but in demand, criminals will supply the product. Prohibition directly led to the strength of organized crime in the United States.

In the 1930s, Prohibition was repealed in the middle of the Great Depression. Strait-laced bureaucrats looking for another target turned their attention to marijuana, which, at the time, was mostly used in the Mexican and black communities. They painted the drug—and the communities using it—as a threat to the already crippled country and began the process of banning it. Twenty-nine states had outlawed marijuana by 1931, and in 1937, the Marijuana Tax Act was passed, essentially making the plant illegal in the United States.

Since then, lawmakers have been doing a do-si-do with the drug. Over the decades, stricter enforcement and the passing of mandatory sentencing laws have traded off with repeals of those laws and efforts at legalization. Today, nine states have legalized marijuana (with 29 allowing medical marijuana), but, as far as the federal government is concerned, the drug is still *cannabis non grata*.[1]

In Britain drugs were not controlled until 1916 when drug use by returning veterans was seen as a problem. It was largely seen as a medical issue. Drugs were available from doctors who prescribed low doses to maintain functioning. The medical use of drugs was separated from the punishment for unregulated drug use. This policy was maintained through the 1960s. Under this policy there was little recreational drug use.

And today we see the relaxing of many of these laws. Marijuana is legal in many states and it is legal in Canada. But other drugs such as opioids and heroin are still illegal. So it is interesting to look at Portugal, where all drugs are legal. It all began with a harm reduction policy that involved a needle exchange program administered by pharmacies.

In Portugal, drug treatment and rehab programs are all sponsored by the government, and include drug substitution programs as well. Results include a 17 percent reduction in AIDS cases and a ninety percent rate drop in drug related HIV infection, along with a decrease in drug usage. As of 2012 Portugal's drug death rate was three per million compared to the EU average of 17.3 per million.[2]

VALUES

Values work in two ways here. One is the values of a society in deciding to outlaw certain types of recreational drugs, supposedly because of the effects they have on people. The second has to do with the consequences of those values. Does outlawing a drug end up having a beneficial or negative effect on both the persons involved and on the society at large? And if not, what alternatives are there, especially if the values of the society deem such drugs as bad? Depending on the findings, the society may have to re-evaluate its values.

LOGIC

Logic, or reasoning, will be used to determine how the information we have fits with the stated values of the society. We will look to see if a specific course of action actually meets or contradicts those values.

DISCUSSION

Here we have a clash of values on different levels. On the one hand societies want to ban substances that are seen as dangerous to people, or the use of which can be seen having negative effects on the society. On the other hand we see a tremendous demand for these substances.

A good example of the problems faced today can be seen by taking a closer look at the prohibition era of the 1920s when alcohol use was prohibited by law.

Various forms of behaviors including alcoholism, family violence and "saloon-based political corruption" led people such as pious Protestants along with social Progressives to ban the production, sale, and importation of alcoholic beverages.

The history of prohibition in the United States dates from the 1820s when the first temperance movement was founded. In 1851 the state of Maine adopted a law banning the manufacture and sale of alcohol. The movement gained in popularity and the Congress that convened in 1917 had a majority of "dries." They argued that the resources that went into the production of alcohol would better be used to serve the war effort.

According to most historians, the ban did work to cut alcohol consumption, and thereby the diseases and problems associated with it. But the demand was still there. Soon speakeasies were proliferating and illegal operations were started.[3]

The main point here, to bring it to today's issues, is that prohibition does not really work. While it may reduce overall consumption it creates other problems.

So let us look at these other problems. We will talk about alcohol and then we will discuss other drugs. Today various groups want to include alcohol as a drug, which, of course, it is. So they tend to say things like alcohol and other drugs.

The biggest problem has to do with the legal aspects of drugs, where drug use, let alone selling, is considered a crime. Therefore, drug users are imprisoned.

According to a poll done for the Center on Addiction, between 1996 and 2006 the U.S. population rose by 12 percent while the prison population rose by 33 percent. The number of inmates jailed because of substance abuse issues rose by 43 percent.

To conduct the study CASA Columbia analyzed data from eleven federal prisons and reviewed more that 650 articles, as well as reviewing standards of treatments. Of the 2.3 million inmates in 2006, 855 were substance involved with 1.5 million meeting the DSM-IV criteria for substance abuse. In 2006 alcohol and other drugs were involved in 78 percent of violent crimes, 83 percent of property crimes and 77 percent of public order, immigration or weapons offense and parole/probation violation. Only 11 percent of all inmates received any kind of treatment.[4]

While drug use and crime seem to go together, looking at cause and effect is problematic. Do people who use drugs commit crimes to get money to support their habits, or does using drugs lead to criminal behaviour?

A report prepared for the Senate of Canada in October of 2001 stated that,

> Illegal drug use is almost automatically associated with criminal behaviour. The statistical relationship between illegal drug use and crime is convincing at first glance, but it is not possible to draw a conclusion regarding a definite cause-and-effect link between the two phenomena. The suggestion that drugs lead to crime ignores the impact that living conditions can have on an individual and takes no account, according to Serge Brochu (an expert in this field), of a body of data showing that most illegal drug users in Canada and elsewhere will never be *regular users*. It bears repeating that drug use is still, for the most part, a sporadic, recreational, exploratory activity. Most people are able to manage their drug use without any difficulty. Very few will become regular users, and even fewer will develop a drug addiction.

The link between criminal activity and drug use is not clear. One point is that a great deal of the crime committed by drug users is to pay for their habits. The more one uses drugs the more one needs to steal to pay for those drugs. "For dependent users, dependency will very often have the effect of increasing their involvement in crime. However, it must be understood that this involvement will to a large extent be determined by their circumstances, the drug they use, their lifestyle, their attraction to certain types of activities, and their economic and social resources"[5]

So where are we? In dealing with drug use there seem to be two basic models. One is to treat the whole issue in terms of criminal behaviour, from manufacture to selling to using while the other is to look at what the causes of drug use are, and at the relationship between drugs and crime. This could lead to a number of different options, from therapeutic ones to harm reduction to a medical model where drug use is seen as a disease that needs to be treated as opposed to a criminal activity that needs to be punished.

If we just deal with using drugs, it is clear that the strict criminal model does not work. People who are jailed for drug use do not get any treatment and can end up back in the same situations they were in that led to their drug use and incarceration. This is what is known as a revolving door policy. Staying just with the users, some kind of treatment program is needed. We can also look at harm reduction models. These models take on a number of different methods. One is to set up safe injection sites that are supervised by medical personnel to ensure that users use clean needles and proper doses. If an overdose happens, trained personnel can resolve the issue.

Another model is a needle exchange program. Users return used needles to a safe place and get clean needles in return.

Neither of these models have to condone drug use—they are simply designed to reduce the harm done by improper taking of drugs and in sharing needles which can lead to spreading diseases. So let us look at some of the statistics to see if these programs actually reduce harm.

In 2003 a safe injection site called Insite was established in Vancouver, British Columbia. As of 2019 there have been 48,798 clinical treatment visits and 6440 overdose interventions without any deaths. A public health emergency was declared in 2016 in response to the opioid crisis. Before the emergency was declared there were thirty overdose interventions a month. After the emergency was called that rose to thirty a day.

The site also provides a needle exchange program which also has a needle pickup program in more remote communities.

A study conducted by the College of Family Physicians of Canada in 2017 found that,

> Best evidence from cohort and modeling studies suggests that SISs are associated with lower overdose mortality (88 fewer overdose deaths per 100 000 person-years [PYs]), 67 percent fewer ambulance calls for treating overdoses, and a decrease in HIV infections.

The study goes on to show that,

- Of persons living within five hundred m of the SIS (70 percent of SIS users), overdose deaths decreased from 253 to 165 per 100,000 PYs and the absolute risk difference was 88 deaths per 100,000 PYs; one overdose death was prevented annually for every 1137 users.
- There was no change in mortality in the rest of city.
- Before the SIS opened, 35 percent of 598 intravenous drug users were admitted to hospital in a three-year period,[2] 15 percent for skin infections.
- After the SIS opened, of 1083 SIS users over 4 years,3 nine percent were admitted with cutaneous injection-related infections (including osteomyelitis and endocarditis).
- While SIS nurse "referral" to hospital increased the likelihood of admission, the average length of stay decreased by eight days (from 12 to four).[3]
- Indirect comparison of different cohorts is a limitation.
- Near one SIS, average monthly ambulance calls with naloxone treatment for suspected opioid overdose decreased from 27 to nine (relative risk reduction of 67 percent).[4]
- About six to 57 HIV infections per year are prevented by the SIS according to mathematical modeling.[5,6]

As these studies show, harm reduction works.

CONCLUSIONS

Metaphysics

The issue here is how to treat alcohol and other drug use. We can criminalize them or look to more therapeutic models such as treating drugs as a medical issue or looking to reduce the harm done by the use of these drugs.

Epistemology

In looking at the information we have regarding drug use and treatment we saw that criminalizing drugs does not work. While criminalizing alcohol and other drugs may reduce their usage, it also causes other problems, such as making criminals out of people who otherwise would not be criminals. It overloads the prison system, and when in prison drug users do not get any help, which adds to the problem rather than solving it.

It also leaves drug sales and distribution in the hands of criminals.

Values

As we saw values operate on two levels. On the one hand the values of a society function to see that such drug use is antithetical to the social values of a given community. On the other hand we saw that criminalizing drugs does not solve the problem in that the consequences of drug use cause more problems than treating usage as a form of criminal behavior.

CONCLUSIONS

One solution is to take all drugs out of the criminal system and look at drug use as a medical issue. Another is to look at trying to ease the negative consequences of drug use by having various harm reduction programs put in place.

This chapter dealt with the usage of alcohol and other drugs. The issue of drug distribution and selling was mentioned only in passing. We should however follow through and look at our conclusions regarding usage and apply it to selling.

If we keep drugs illegal, then selling and distributing drugs will also be kept illegal, and nothing will be solved. But harm reduction models could then be put into place. If we legalize drugs, as some jurisdictions have done with marijuana, then we could also legalize the selling and distribution of drugs. For example, when prohibition ended, some jurisdictions went to a private sector model, where the manufacture, distribution and selling was left to private business. Some jurisdictions left the production of alcoholic products in the private sector but maintained government run retail stores. This could also be a model for drugs such as marijuana. When it comes to so-called hard drugs, such as heroin and opiates, some kind of medical model should probably be used, so doctors could regulate dosages. Here we have to be careful that doctors do not over prescribe these drugs, and drug manufacturers must be straightforward about the nature of the drugs they produce.

NOTES

1. Allison McNearney, "The Complicated History of Cannabis," History.com, A&E Television Networks, April 20, 2018, https://www.history.com/news/marijuana-criminalization-reefer-madness-history-flashback. Site checked July 31, 2020.

2. Susana Ferreira, "Portugal's Radical Drugs Policy is Working. Why Hasn't the World Copied it?" December 05, 2017, The Guardian.com. https://www.theguardian.com/news/2017/dec/05/portugals-radical-drugs-policy-is-working-why-hasnt-the-world-copied-it site checked July 31, 2020.

3. Jeffrey A. Miron and Jeffrey Zwiebel, "Alcohol Consumption During Prohibition," NBER Working Papers Series, The National Bureau of Economic Research. April 1991, https://www.nber.org/papers/w3675.pdf site checked July 31, 2020.

4. Partnership staff, "Substance Abuse and America's Prison Population 2010," Partnership to End Addiction, February 2010, https://www.drugfree.org/reports/behind-bars-ii-substance-abuse-and-america's-prison-population. Site checked July 31, 2020.

5. "Final Report: Cannabis; Our Position for Canadian Public Policy," Senate Canada, Government of Canada September 16, 2002, https://sencanada.ca/en/Commitees/ille/37-1. Site checked July 31.2020.

6. Kathleen Dooling MD MPH and Michael Rachliss MD LLD, "Vancouver's Supervised Injection Facility Challenges Canada's Drug Laws," National Institutes of Health, September 21, 2010, https://www.ncbi.nlm.nih.gov/pmc/articles/PMC2942917. Site checked July 31, 2020.

Chapter Nine

The Teaching of Art

METAPHYSICS

I see the teaching of the arts and humanities as a moral issue in that these subjects are important for a number of reasons. One is that the arts are an important part of our culture and as such should be taught in schools. Another is that the humanities, subjects such as literature, history and even civics and political science, should be taught so that people can become well-informed citizens.

On the other side there appear to be two separate reasons for not teaching the arts. One is that the arts cannot be quantified and are thus seen by some economists as superficial and having no place in a proper curriculum. A second reason is political. Various political leaders of all stripes see art as a challenge to authority, and often try to belittle both art and artists. We have seen this kind of behavior in leaders from Hitler to Stalin to Pinochet. To a lesser extent, we see it in the United States and Canada.

Hitler saw abstract art as degenerate and labelled the artists, whether Jewish or communist, as degenerates. He, and those close to him, knew that art could play a role in the rise or fall of a dictatorship. Stalin went further and executed artists who went afoul of the state rules. In Chile under Pinochet muralists were arrested.

In more developed countries today we see the arts as the first subject to be cut from academic curricula. In the province of Ontario, Canada, the current government cut ten million dollars from the arts program, putting many arts programs in schools at risk. In the United States the Trump government put forward a budget proposal that would eliminate the National Endowment for the Arts.

142   Chapter Nine

The question becomes one of looking at the importance of the arts in both education and in the society at large.

EPISTEMOLOGY

Here we must find information about the arts to see if they are in fact important in education and in society at large.

I would like to begin by offering a definition of art that I presented in my book, *Art Matters: The Knowledge of Art/The Art of Knowledge*. The definition is twofold. First I offer a brief set of criteria for something that is called art must meet. These criteria are:

1. Art works are designed to get people to react by appealing to our senses;
2. Art is a form of cultural and historical expression;
3. Art is a value laden problem-solving enterprise;
4. Art is a form of knowledge.[1]

The second part of the definition has to do with elaborating on the last two points. In that book I compare art to science in that new art forms develop, at least in part, because the old form has run its course and nothing new can be done in it. Much new art is an experiment to see what will work. This is true of abstract forms as well as going back to older forms and modernizing them.

In their work artists express how they perceive the world. Poets use imaginative language, novelists use prose, painters use visual imagery. But in all cases, something is being expressed. In order to understand what is being expressed we have to learn the proper language.

For example, when someone sees an abstract painting their response might be, "What is it supposed to be?" The point is that it is abstract and is not supposed to represent anything. But in order to know this, the viewer must know something about the nature of abstract painting.[2]

On this view art is important because it is part of our culture.

On the side of teaching art in school the Institute did an empirical study,

> We recently conducted the first ever large-scale, randomized controlled trial study of a city's collective efforts to restore arts education through community partnerships the impacts of enriching arts field trip experiences, this study examines the effects of a and investments. Building on our previous investigations of sustained reinvigoration of schoolwide arts education. Specifically, our study focuses on the initial two years of Houston's Arts Access Initiative and includes 42 elementary and middle schools with over 10,000 third- through eighth-grade

students. Our study was made possible by generous support of the Houston Endowment, the National Endowment for the Arts, and the Spencer Foundation.

They found that,

> We find that a substantial increase in arts educational experiences has remarkable impacts on students' academic, social, and emotional outcomes. Relative to students assigned to the control group, treatment school students experienced a 3.6 percentage point reduction in disciplinary infractions, an improvement of 13 percent of a standard deviation in standardized writing scores, and an increase of eight percent of a standard deviation in their compassion for others. In terms of our measure of compassion for others, students who received more arts education experiences are more interested in how other people feel and more likely to want to help people who are treated badly.

And they conclude,

> As education policymakers increasingly rely on empirical evidence to guide and justify decisions, advocates struggle to make the case for the preservation and restoration of K-12 arts education. To date, there is a remarkable lack of large-scale experimental studies that investigate the educational impacts of the arts. One problem is that U.S. school systems rarely collect and report basic data that researchers could use to assess students' access and participation in arts educational programs. Moreover, the most promising outcomes associated with arts education learning objectives extend beyond commonly reported outcomes such as math and reading test scores. There are strong reasons to suspect that engagement in arts education can improve school climate, empower students with a sense of purpose and ownership, and enhance mutual respect for their teachers and peers. Yet, as educators and policymakers have come to recognize the importance of expanding the measures we use to assess educational effectiveness, data measuring social and emotional benefits are not widely collected. Future efforts should continue to expand on the types of measures used to assess educational program and policy effectiveness.3

On the other side, there are a number of reasons given to eliminate art teaching in schools.

In his blog on the Phi Delta Kappan site, Danny Gregory, on August 24, 2018, writes:

> In the lower grades, kids just have fun drawing and painting. They don't really need much encouragement or instruction. In middle school, the majority start to lose their passion for making stuff and instead learn the price of making mistakes. All too often, art class becomes a gut, an opportunity for adolescents to screw around. By high school, they have been divided into a handful who are

"artsy" and may go on to art school and the vast majority who have no interest in art at all.

In short, every child starts out with a natural interest in art, but for most it is slowly drained away until all that's left is a handful of teens in eyeliner and black clothing whose parents worry they'll never move out of the basement.

Here's a modest proposal: Let's take the "art" out of "art education."

"Art" is not respected in this country. It's seen as frivolity, an indulgence, a way to keep kids busy with scissors and paste. "Art" is an elitist luxury that hard-nosed bureaucrats know they can cut with impunity. And so they do, making math and science the priority to fill the ranks of future bean-counters and pencil pushers.

So I propose we get rid of "art" education and replace it with something that is crucial to the future of our world: creativity.

He goes on to argue:

Nowadays, we all need to be creative in ways that we never did, or could, before. Solving problems, using tools, collaborating, expressing our ideas clearly, being entrepreneurial and resourceful—these are the skills that matter in the twenty-first-century, post-corporate labor market. Instead of being defensive about art, instead of talking about culture and self-expression, we have to focus on the power of creativity and the skills required to develop it. A great artist is also a problem solver, a presenter, an entrepreneur, a fabricator, and more.[4]

In another blog called Why Art Classes Should be Cut, the blogger Caleb argues,

The best argument in favor for cutting art classes and programs from schools is that it will force students to focus more on core classes. It is more important for students to do well in classes like math, science, and writing, rather than classes that students take to express creativity.[5]

VALUES

Here we see a clash of values, one sees the value of art instruction, and of the arts in general, and the other does not.

The view that sees the arts as valuable has two points. One is that the arts themselves have value, they are part of our culture, and as such should be taught. The second point is that the teaching of art has valuable consequences for other aspects of the students' lives.

The other view does not see the value of art teaching, especially if it interferes with students learning the core curriculum.

LOGIC

So we will use logic to see which view stands up to argument.

DISCUSSION

Given that I have written positively about art, it should be clear that I am in favour of keeping art in schools, both to teach art and to teach the history of art so people can come to understand new developments. But to be a good philosopher, I must be able to meet the opposing arguments.

The two main arguments against the teaching of art are educational and economic.

The main arguments here are cost factors and that arts teaching takes students away from their core curricula which contains the important subjects. Often these arguments go hand in hand as economics are used to justify the reduction of art teaching.

But as we have seen, art teaching actually adds to students' abilities to do other subjects, and has a lasting effect on their adult lives.

The importance of teaching art in schools is not just about art, but is about teaching creativity, which is what blogger Danny Gregory argues. It is a great idea to teach creativity, but one needs a base to teach creativity from. And that base can be art. That is any art form, from painting and sculpting to music to poetry. So the teaching of art does in fact develop creativity. Students also need to be taught how to abstract their creative thinking to other areas. And this does involve critical thinking. One aspect of critical thinking is problem solving. And, as I argued above, one aspect of art is that it is a form of problem solving. Thus the teaching of art is justified.

CONCLUSION

Metaphysics

The issue is one of whether or not to teach art in schools. We presented positions on both sides of the issue.

Epistemology

We saw that empirical studies actually demonstrate the benefits of teaching art in school.

Values

Values work in a number of ways. The social values for or against teaching art were presented. But the real role of values is in looking at the consequences of teaching art. As was demonstrated above in the study done by the Brookings Institute, the teaching of art has tremendous benefits, from an artistic standpoint and from an economic standpoint.

Logic

So logic compels us to conclude that the benefits of teaching art in school far outweighs any argument to take art out of school. And the main reason is that art matters.

NOTES

1. Koenig, Bernard, *Art Matters*: *The Art of Knowledge, the Knowledge of Art*, (Palo Alto: Academica Press, 2009) 241.
2. Koenig, 240.
3. Kisida, Brian and Daniel H. Bowen, "New Evidence of the Benefits of Arts Education" Brookings Institution. February 12, 2019, https://www.brookings.edu/blog/brown-center-chalkboard/2019/02/12/new-evidence-of-the-benefits-of-arts-education. Site checked July 31 2020.
4. Danny Gregory, "Let's Get Rid of Art Education in Schools," Phi Delta Kappa, April 15, 2016, https://www.dannygregorysblog.com/2016/04/15/lets-get-rid-of-art-education-in-schools. Site checked July 31, 2020.
5. Caleb Chavis, "Why Art Classes Should be Cut," Medium.com, April 29, 2016, https://www.medium.com/@calcha57/why-art-classes-should-be-cut-479dc8ed6f56. Site checked July 31, 2020.

Concluding Remarks

In books such as this one, the format is to first tell the readers what is going to be done. Then the body of the book does that. In the conclusion the author tells the reader what has been done.

In this book I have tried to demonstrate a method for solving moral issues. The method involves the range of philosophy. We must first clearly define the issue at hand—what leads to the controversy? Once we have a sense of what we are trying to resolve we need the relevant information to apply to the problem. Then we look at our values. As has been demonstrated, values come from our culture. And, in a very significant sense, we live in many cultures. We have knowledge of science, of religion, of social backgrounds and so on. We have seen that many moral conflicts arise from two sources. One is how new knowledge challenges old beliefs, and the second is how different cultures have different values.

Culture must be seen in broad terms. Different cultures may represent different countries of origin, different religions, different knowledge bases. And as we have seen, cultural belief can be so strong as to deny relevant or new knowledge.

But while we all have different beliefs we also must look critically at those beliefs. It is one thing to provide a reason for one's beliefs, it is another to be able to offer a justification for that reason.

It is important that when looking at moral conflicts, we are careful to look at what the conflict is, where it comes from, and why it exists. Then we must apply the relevant knowledge to the issue in order to properly resolve the conflict.

In carefully defining an issue and in carefully spelling out the values involved, and then by applying the relevant knowledge, perhaps some of these issues can be resolved. For example, most religions oppose abortion, yet we also see religious groups challenging the traditional thinking of religions on that and related issues around fertility and sexuality. Traditional thinking opposes euthanasia. But such thinking is all too often based on outmoded conceptions of what it means to be alive, and how medical technologies work.

And it is not just religion that opposes many ideas but old traditions and old customs also come into play. Also, in many countries, religion is used to justify cultural beliefs. While we want to hold onto our traditional beliefs, we may have to look hard at new developments in appropriate fields of knowledge and use that knowledge to critically look at our traditions.

There are many issues this book did not look at, including the current negative views of science regarding health care issues, such as being opposed to vaccinations. Yet people who hold these views accept science in other walks of life, so why do they reject science when it comes to health? By carefully defining the issue and by looking at the relevant knowledge, and by assessing how values function, people may come to change their positions.

What I have been describing, and what I have been doing, can be called critical thinking. And that is the ultimate lesson of this book. Don't just accept a viewpoint on an issue, but look at what the issue is, why that view is being proffered, bring the relevant information to bear on the issue, and critically evaluate the values involved. The whole process is one of reasoning, so logic is always being used.

So ultimately the lesson of this book is to get you to think critically about moral issues.

Bibliography

"5 Facts About the Abortion Debate in America," Fact Tank, Pew Research, August 30, 2019, www.pewresearch/fact-tank/2019/08/30/facts-about-abortion-in-america.

"About our Work," Catholics for Choice, https://www.catholicsforchoice.org/about-us/about-our-work.

Ahmad, Imad-ad-Dean," On Natural Law and Shari'ah" Delivered August 3, 2009, Institute to the Institute of Freedom's Summer Institute, www.Minaret.org site checked on February 3, 2020.

Aquinas, Thomas, *Summa Theologica*. London, Blackfriars, 1963. Translation led by His Eminence Michael Cardinal Browne and the Most Reverend father Anticeto Fernandez.

Aristotle, *The Basic Works of Aristotle*, Edited by Richard Mckeon, (New York: Random House, 1941).

Bagemihl, Bruce, *Biological Exuberance*: *Animal Homosexuality and Natural Diversity*, (New York: Saint Martin's Press, 1999).

Banerjee, Abhijit V., and Esther Duflo, *Good Economics for Hard Times*, (New York: hard Times, 2019).

Belenky, Mary Field, Clinchy, Blythe McVIcker, Golderberger, Nancy Rule and Tarule, Jill Mattuck, *Women's Ways of Knowing*: *The Development of Self, Voice and Mind*. (New York: Basic Books, 1986).

Bentham, Jeremy, *An Introduction to the Principles of Morals and legislation*, in Steven M. Cahn and Peter Markie, eds, *Ethics*: *History, Theory and Contemporary Issues* (New York: Oxford University Press, 1998).

"Canadian Abortion Rights Action League (CARAL)," Rise Up! A Digital Archive of Feminist Activism, Digitizing Feminist Activism, https://www.riseupfeministarchive.ca/activism/organizations/canadian-abortion-rights-action-league-caral.

Canadian Medical Association Policy on Induced Abortion, Canadian Medical Association, December 1988, https://www.personhood.ca/pdfs/cma_policy.pdf.

Canadian Multiculturalism Act–R.S.C., 1985, c. 24 (4th Supp.) (Section 3), Justice Laws Website. Government of Canada, 1985, https://www.laws-lois.justice.gc.ca/eng/acts//c-18.7/page-1.htm#h-73130.

"Catechism of the Catholic Church," The Vatican, https://www.Vatican.va/archive/ccc_css/archive/catechism/p3s2 c2a5.htm\.

"The Causes of Climate Change," Global Climate Change, NASA, https://www.climate.nasa.gov/causes/.

"The Changing Face of the Country," Spiegel International website. Spiegel International. April 19, 2018, www.spiegel.de/international/germany/germany-ans-immigration-the-changing-face-of-the-country.

Chavis, Caleb, "Why Art Classes Should be Cut," Medium.com, April 29, 2016, https://www.medium.com/@calcha57/why-art-classes-should-be-cut-479dc8ed6f56.

Chodorow, Nancy, *The Reproduction of Mothering: Psychoanalysis and the Sociology of Gender*, (Berkeley: University of California Press, 1978).

"Climate Change: How do we Know?" Global Climate Change, NASA, https://www.climate.nasa.gov/evidence/.

Cohen, Stephen J. and Bradford DeLong, *Concrete Economics*: *The Hamilton Approach to Economic Growth and Policy*, (Cambridge: Harvard Business Review Press, 2016).

Collins, Patricia Hill, *Black Feminist Thought*: *Consciousness and the Politics of Empowerment*, (New York: Routledge, 1991).

Daly, Markate, ed. *Communitarianism*: *A New Public Ethics*, (Belmont: Wadsworth, 1993).

Darwin, Charles, *The Origin of Species*, (New York: Mentor, 1958).

De Haas, Hein, Stephen Castles and Mark J. Miller, *The Age of Migration* companion 4th edition website, Chapter 12.3. Macmillan Publishers Ltd. www.age-of-migration.com/uk/casestudies. "Multiculturalism Policies in Contemporary Democracies United States," Multiculturalism Policy Index, Queens University. https://www.queensu.ca.mcp/immigrant-minorities/evidence/united-states.

Dooling, Kathleen MD MPH and Michael Rachliss MD LLD, "Vancouver's Supervised Injection Facility Challenges Canada's Drug Laws," National Institutes of Health, September 21, 2010, https://www.ncbi.nlm.nih.gov/pmc/articles/PMC2942917.

Draper, Patricia, "!Kung Women: Contrasts in Sexual Egalitarianism in Foraging and Sedentary Contexts" in *Towards and Anthropology of Women*, edited by Rayna Reiter, (New York: Monthly Review Press, 1975).

Durisin, Elya M, Emily van der Meulen, Chris Bruckert. *Red Light Labour*: *Sex Work*, *Regulation, Agency and Resistance*. (Vancouver: UBC Press, 2018).

"Dutch Politician Pim Fortuyn Assassinated," The Guardian website. Guardian News & Media Ltd., May 06, 2002, https://www.theguardian.com/world/2002/may/06/3.

Easton, Thomas A, Durisin, Elya M, Emily van der Meulen, Chris Bruckert. *Red Light Labour*: *Sex Work*, *Regulation, Agency and Resistance*. (Vancouver: UBC Press, 2018).

"Euthanasia, Assisted Suicide and Non-Resuscitation on Request," Government of the Netherlands, https://www.government.nl/topics/euthanasia/euthanasia-assisted-suicide-and-non-resuscitation-on-request.

Ewing, Eve. L. *New York Times*, April 6, 2017.
Fakhry, Majid, *A History of Islamic Philosophy*. (New York: Columbia University press, 1970).
Ferreira, Susana, "Portugal's Radical Drugs Policy is Working. Why Hasn't the World Copied it?" December 05, 2017, The Guardian.com. https://www.theguardian.com/news/2017/dec/05/portugals-radical-drugs-policy-is-working-why-hasnt-the-world-copied-it.
"Final Report: Cannabis; Our Position for Canadian Public Policy," Senate Canada, Government of Canada September 16,2002, https://sencanada.ca/en/Commitees/ille/37-1.
Fine, Cordelia. *Testosterone Rex: Myths of Sex, Science and Society*, (London: W.W. Norton, 2017).
Firestone, Shulamith, *The Dialectic of Sex: The Case for Feminist Revolution* (New York: Farrar Strauss Geroux, 1970).
Fletcher, Joseph, "Infanticide and the Ethics of Loving Concern," in Kohl.
Fox, Robin, *The Red Lamp of Incest* (New York: E.P. Dutton. 1980).
Freud, Sigmund, "A Note on the Unconscious, in *General Psychological Theory*, ed by Rieff, Phillip, (New York: Collier Books, 1963).
Freud, Sigmund, "Female Sexuality" in *The Sexuality of Love*, edited by Philip Reiff, (New York: Collier Books, 1963).
Freud, Sigmund, "The Passing of the Oedipus Complex" in *Sexuality and the Psychology of Love*. Edited by Philip Reiff, (New York: Collier Books, 1963).
Freud, Sigmund, *Civilization and its Discontents*, Translated by Joan Riviere, (London: Hogarth Press, 1962).
Freud, Sigmund, *Totem and Taboo*, Translated by James Strachey,(New York,: W.W. Norton, 1962).
Freud, Sigmund, "The Unconscious," in *General Psychological Theory* ed by Phillip Rieff, (New York: Collier Books, 1963).
Friedan, Betty, *The Feminine Mystique*, (New York: Dell, 1964).
Galbraith, John Kenneth, *A Brief History of Financial Euphoria,* (New York: Whittle Books, 1994).
Gilligan, Carol, *In a Different Voice: Psychological theory and Women's Development*, (Cambridge: Harvard University Press, 1982).
Greer, Germaine, *The Female Eunuch*, (New York: Harper, 2008).
Gregory, Danny, "Let's Get Rid of Art Education in Schools," Phi Delta Kappa, April 15, 2016, https://www.dannygregorysblog.com/2016/04/15/lets-get-rid-of-art-education-in-schools.
Grimshaw, Jean, *Philosophy and Feminist Thinking*, (Minneapolis: University of Minnesota Press, 1986).
Harris, Marvin, *Cannibals and Kings: The Origins of Culture*, (New York: Random House, 1987).
Hodgson, Bernard, *Economics as Moral Science*, (Berlin: Springer, 2001).
Hodgson, Bernard, ed. *The Invisible Hand and the Common Good*, (Berlin: Springer, 2004).
hooks, bell, *Talking Back: thinking feminist, thinking black*, (Toronto: Between the Lines, 1989).

Hume, David, *An Inquiry Concerning Human Understanding*, ed by I.A. Selby-Bigg, (Oxford: The Clarendon Press, 1967).

"Inadequate Food Distribution Systems," Mission 2014: Feeding the World, 2014, http://12.000.scripts.mit.edu/mission2014/problems/inadequate-food-distribution-systems.

IPCC AR5 WG1 Summary for Policymakers 2013, p.17.

Jablonka, Eva and Marion J. Lamb, Evolution in Four Dimensions: Genetic, Epigenetic, Behavioural, and Symbolic Variations in the History of Life, (Cambridge: MIT Press, 2005).

Jacob, Francois, *The Logic of Life*: *A History of Heredity*, (New York: Vintage Books, 1976).

Jones, Marianne and Ranjeet Mohini, *Multiculturism*: *Perspectives and Overview*, (Middletown Delaware 2017).

Kant, Immanuel, *Foundations of the Metaphysics of Morals*, translated by Lewis White beck, (Indianapolis, The Liberal Arts Press, 1959).

Kisida, Brian and Daniel H. Bowen, "New Evidence of the Benefits of Arts Education" Brookings Institution. February 12, 2019, https://www.brookings.edu/blog/brown-center-chalkboard/2019/02/12/new-evidence-of-the-benefits-of-arts-education.

Koenig, Berard, *Art Matters*: *The Art of Knowledge*, *the Knowledge of Art*, (Palo Alto: Academica Press, 2009).

Koenig, Bernie, *Natural law*, *Science*, *and the Social Construction of Reality*, Lanham, University Press of America, 2009.

Kohl, Marvin, ed. *Infanticide and the Value of Life*, (Buffalo: Prometheus Books, 1978) Kohlberg, Lawrence, "How Moral are You?" in Hock, Roger, *Forty Studies that Changed Psychology*, (Englewood Cliffs: Prentice Hall, 1992).

Kreet, Peter, *Three Approaches to Abortion*, (San Francisco: Ignatius Press 2002)

Kymlicka, Will. *Contemporary Political Philosophy*: *An Introduction* (Oxford: Clarendon Press, 1990).

LaFollette, ed. Ethics in Practice: An Anthology, 4 ed. (Oxford: Wiley and Sons, 2014).

Lanahan, Sean, "Debunking the Over-population Myth," in Easton.

Leacock, Stephen, Elements of Political Science, (Boston: Houghton Mifflin 1921).

Lerner, Michael, *Surplus Powerlessness*, (Oakland: The Institute for Labor and Mental health, 1986).

Locke, John, An Essay Concerning The True original Extent and End of Civil Government, in Barker, Sir Ernest, *The Social Contract*, (London: Oxford University Press, 1960).

Marquis, Don, "An argument that Abortion is Wrong," in Lafollette.

Maslow, Abraham, *Towards a Psychology of Being*, (Sublime Books, 2014).

Mchale, Kolby. *Gun Ownership*: *The Right to Bear Arms and the Surrounding Controversy*.

McNearney, Allison, "The Complicated History of Cannabis," History.com, A&E Television Networks, April 20, 2018, https://www.history.com/news/marijuana-criminalization-reefer-madness-history-flashback.

"Medical Assistance in Dying," Health Canada, Government of Canada, June 2016, https://www.canada.ca/en/health-canada-services/medical-assistance-dying.

Mill, John Stuart, *Utilitarianism,* in Cahn and Markie.

Millet, Kate, *Sexual Politics* (New York: Columbia University Press, 1970).

Miron, Jeffrey A., and Jeffrey Zwiebel, "Alcohol Consumption During Prohibition," NBER Working Papers Series, The National Bureau of Economic Research. April 1991, https://www.nber.org/papers/w3675.pdf.

Moi, Toril, ed. *The Kristeva Reader*, (New York: The Columbia University Press, 1986).

Montague, Ashley, *The Nature of Human Aggression*, (New York: Oxford University Press, 1971).

"Multiculturalism Policies in Contemporary Democracies Netherlands," Multiculturalism Policy Index, Queens University, https://www.queensu.ca/mcp/immigrant-minorities/evidence/netherlands.

"NASA, NOAA Data Show 2016 Warmest Year on Record Globally," NASA News and Feature Releases, Goddard Institute for Space Studies, NASA, January 18, 2017, http://www.giss.nasa.gov/research/news/20170118/.

Painter, Carla Valle, "Sense of Belonging: Literature Review," Statistics Canada, Government of Canada, June 2013. https://www.canada.ca/en/immigration-refugees-citizenship/corporate/reports-statistics.

Partnership staff, "Substance Abuse and America's Prison Population 2010," Partnership to End Addiction, February 2010, https://www.drugfree.org/reports/behind-bars-ii-substance-abuse-and-america's-prison-population.

Piaget, Jean, *The Language and Thought of the Child*, translated by Marjorie and Ruth Gabain, (New York: Simon and Schuster, 1965).

Polanyi, Karl, *The Great Transformation*: *The Political and Economic origins or our Time*, (Boston, Beacon Press, 2001).

Popper, Sir Karl, *Conjectures and Refutations*, (London: Routledge and Kegan Paul, 1965).

Rand, Ayn, *Atlas Shrugged* New York: Plume reprint, 1999).

Ringdal, Nils Johan, *Love For Sale*: *A World History of Prostitution*, Translated by Richard Daly, (New York: Grove Press, 2004).

Rippon, Gina, "Do Women and Men Have Different Brains?" in *New Scientist*, Vol 241, no 3219, 2 March 2019.

Rocca, Corrine, *New Scientist*, 18 January 2020.

Schrupp, Antje, *A Brief History of Feminism*, (Cambridge,: MIT Press, 2017).

Sellars, Wilfrid, Science, Perception, and Reality. (London: Routledge and Kegan Paul, 1963).

"Should Euthanasia or Physician-Assisted Suicide be Legal?" Britannica ProCon, https://www.euthanasia.procon.org.

Smith, Adam, *The Theory of Moral Sentiments*, in Heilbroner, Robert, ed, *The Essential Adam Smith,* (New York: W.W. Norton, 1987).

Smith, Adam, *The Wealth of Nations*, in Heilbroner: *Special Action Programme to Combat Forced Labour* (20 May 2014)."(PDF). International Labour Organization.

"Summary for Policymakers," Intergovernmental Panel on Climate Change, United Nations, February 2019 www.ipcc.ch/site/assets/uploads/sites/2/2019/05/SR15_SPM_version_report_LR.pdf.

"Teen Birth Rate by State," National Center for Health Statistics, Centers for Disease Control and Prevention. https://www.cdc.gov/nchs/pressroom/sosmap/teen-births/teenbirths.htm.

Thomson, Judith Jarvis, "A Defense of Abortion" in Lafollette.

Unesco website. Unesco. www.eolss.net/Sample-Chapters/C09/E6-156-01-00.pdf.

Warren, Mary Ann, "On The Moral and Legal Status of Abortion." in Lafollette.

Washington, Haydn and Cook, John. *Climate Change Denial: Heads in the Sand* (London: Earthscan, 2011).

"What the Data Says About Gun Deaths in the U.S." Fact Tank, Pew Research, August 16, 2019, https://www.pewresearch.org/fact-tank/2019,08/16/what-the-data-says about-gun-deaths-in-the-u-s/.

Williamson, Linda, Infanticide: "An Anthropological Analysis," in Kohl.

Index

Adam, 59
Adam, Juliette, 68
Ahmad, Imad-ad-Dean, 5
Aquinas, Saint Thomas, 54, 73
Arendt, Hannah, x
Aristotle, 4, 5, 6, 33, 37
Asherites, 4
Augustine, Saint 103

Bagemihl, Bruce, 73
Banerjee, Abhijit, V, 29, 30
Bateman, Angus, 64
Baudelaire, Charles, 104
BEAVER, 107
Belenky, Mary Field, 73
Bentham, Jeremy, 7, 8, 9, 22, 26, 32, 33
Brown, Harvey, x
Bruckert, Chris, 165
Burke, Edmund, 67
Butler, Josephine, 104

Caleb, 144
Canadian Abortion Rights Action League, 82, 83
Canadian Medical Association, 83
Carson, Rachel, 115
CASH, 107

Catholics for Choice, 81, 82
Chance, M.R, 60
Chernobyl, 115
China, 126
Chodorow, Nancy, 11, 36, 71, 72, 73
Christianity, 4, 6, 66, 103
Code of Hammurabi, 100
Cohen, Stephen S, 23
Communitarianism, ix, 21, 22, 23, 34, 37, 38
Copernicus, Nicolai, 6, 36
COYOTE, 105, 107

Daly, Markate, 21, 24,
Darwin, Charles, 15, 16, 17, 60, 64
De Beuuvoir, Simone, 70
de Gouges, Olympe, 67
DeLong, Bradford J, 23
Demar, Claire, 67
De Pizan, Christine, 66
Diotima, 66
Dohm, Hedwig, 69
Douglass, Frederick, 68
Draper, Patricia, 20, 62
Duflo, Esther, 29, 30
Durisin, Elya M, 105

Easton, Thomas, 119
England, 69, 70, 104, 126, 127, 130

Ethics, 2, 10, 12, 21, 36, 82, 96, 105
Ethics of care, 10, 12, 36

Facastoro, Giolamo, 103
Fakhry, Majid, 4
Fine, Cordelia, 62
Fox, Robin, 59,
Francis, Richard, 64
Freud, Sigmund, 11, 15, 16, 17, 18, 20, 21, 59, 60, 62, 71, 75, 108
Friedan, Betty, 70
Fukushima, 115

Galbraith, John Kenneth, 29
Galileo, Galelei, 36
Galloway, Patricia, 64
Genesis, 113
Germany, 46, 47, 48, 53, 56, 69, 129
Gilligan, Carol, 10, 11, 12, 73
Goody, Jack, 60
Gospel of Mary, 66, 103
Greer, Germaine, 70
Gregory, Danny, 143, 145
Grimshaw, Jean, 36, 71
Guide for the Perplexed, 5

Harris, Marvin, 15, 18, 19, 20, 21, 60, 61, 62, 85
Heilbroner, Robert, 32
Hill, Patricia, 70
Hitler, Adolf, 46, 141
Hodgson, Bernard, 29
Holland, 97
hooks, bell, 70
Hrdy, Sarah, Blaffer, 64
Hume, David, 7, 8, 26, 32, 33

Incest, 59
Insite, 138
Irigaray, Lucy, 70
Islam, ix, 3, 4, 5

Jacob, Francois, 16
Jefferson, Thomas, 68
Judaism, ix, 3, 4, 5

Kahn, Ummni, 106
Kant, Immanuel, 10, 12, 35
Kohlberg, Lawrence, 11
Kreet, Peter, 88
Kristeva, Julia, 70
Kuhn, Thomas, 36
Kymlicka, Will, 22, 23, 34

Lanahan, Sean, 121
Leacock, Stephen, ix, 28
Lee-Jarvis, May, x
Lerner, Michael, 34
Leviticus, 58
Libertarianism, 22, 30, 34
Lilith, 59
Locke, John, 7, 8, 15, 23, 25, 30, 31, 32, 33, 102, 127

Magdalene, Mary, 66, 103
Maimonides, Moses, 5, 6
Malthus, Thomas, 19, 20, 61, 85, 121
Manet, Edouard, 104
Manon Lescault, 104
Marks, Jonathon, 64
Marquis, Don, 88
Maslow, Abraham, 35, 71
McDonald v Chicago, 127
Menander, 66
Mendel, Gregor, 16
Mill, Harriet Taylor, 9, 69
Mill, John Stuart, 69
Millett, Kate, 70
Montague, Ashley, 19
Morgentaler, Doctor Henry, 82
Moses, 6, 100
Mott, Lucrezia, 68
Musson, Paddy, x
Mu'tazilites, 4

NASA, 116, 118, 122
National Rifle Association, 128, 130
Natural law, ix, x, 1, 4, 5, 6, 12, 15, 22, 33, 55
Newton, Isaac, 37

Index

Nietzsche, Frederick, 35
Noachid Commandment, 58

Patu, 66
Paul, Saint, 66
Piaget, Jean, 11
Pinochet, Augusto, 141
Plato, 4, 66
Polanyi ,Karl, 26, 27, 28
Porete, Marguerite, 66

Rand, Ayn, 35
Redwood, River, 106
Ringdal, Nils Johan, 100, 102, 103, 104
Rippon, Gina, 63, 64, 65
Robinson Crusoe, 31

Saint-Simon, Henri de, 67, 68
Schrupp, Antje, 66
Scott, Valerie, 105
Second Amendment, 125, 126, 127, 128, 129, 30
Sellars, Wilfrid, 3, 26, 36
Shelley, Mary, 67
Smith, Adam, 8, 26, 27, 28, 32
Snyder, Brian, 64
Social Contract Theory, 7, 12, 15, 23, 30, 31, 33
Socrates, 9, 66

St. James, Margo, 105
Stalin, Josef, 141
Stanton, Elizabeth Cady, 68
Switzerland, 70, 126, 128, 130

Taylor Helen, 69
The Church of the Latter Day Saints, 134
Testosterone, 62, 63, 65, 74
Three Mile Island, 115
Theory, ix, x, 2, 3, 4, 7, 8, 9, 10, 12, 15, 16, 17, 21, 22, 23, 25, 26, 27, 28, 29, 30, 33, 35, 36, 37, 51, 55, 71, 109
Totem and Taboo, 59, 62
Travis, Carol, 64

Utilitarianism, 9, 10, 22, 35

Von Bingen, Hildegard, 66

War, 19, 20, 21, 23, 27, 35, 42, 46, 53, 55, 56, 61, 62, 70, 85, 86, 100
Warren, Mary Ann, 87
Wilhelmina of Milan, 66
Williamson, Laila, 85
Wollstonecraft, Mary, 67

Zola, Emile, 104

About the Author

Bernie Koenig is a retired professor of music and philosophy from Fanshawe College in London, Ontario, Canada. As a philosopher, he is the author of *Natural Law, Science, and the Social Construction of Reality*, and *Art Matters: The Knowledge of Art/The Art of Knowledge*. As a musician he can be heard on two CDs: *Overheard Conversations* and *Three Way Conversations*. Bernie can be contacted at Bernie.koenig@yahoo.ca.

www.ingramcontent.com/pod-product-compliance
Lightning Source LLC
Chambersburg PA
CBHW032105300426
44116CB00007B/891